Where is Taro?
Teacher's Kit

Elizabeth Claire

HARCOURT BRACE

ESL/EFL

Harcourt Brace & Company

Orlando San Diego New York

Toronto London Sydney Tokyo

Consulting Director: Marilyn Rosenthal
Project Editor: Kathleen Schultz
Copy Editor: Rebecca Rauff
Production Manager: Anne Burkett
Design and Production: David Corona, David Corona Design
Film Preparation: Lanman Lithotech
Illustrators: Morissa Lipstein, Loretta Lustig
Cover Illustration: Loretta Lustig
Cover Design: Amy Weisgerber, Success by Design, Inc.

Printed in the United States of America

ISBN: 0–15–599430–1

5 6 7 8 9 0 1 2 022 9 8 7 6 5 4 3 2 1

• • • • • • • •

*This Teacher's Kit is dedicated
to any teacher who has ever been lost
in a multilevel classroom
without a multilevel textbook.*

Elizabeth Claire

• • • • • • • •

Contents

MULTILEVEL QUESTION BANKS AND ACTIVITIES   14

Acknowledgments

The *Where Is Taro? Teacher's Kit* was called forth by Dr. Marilyn Rosenthal, who created exacting specifications for a teacher-friendly format chock-full of usable activities. I owe her profound thanks and appreciation for her vision and wisdom.

Very special extra thanks go to Kathleen Schultz, who helped hone each detail of the kit's content, organization, and wording. Kathleen's patience and clarity in overseeing the project's zillion details inspired and encouraged me through many long, lonely nights at the computer.

Thanks for the professional crucible, TESOL, that offers a forum for researchers, teachers, writers, and publishers to meet, exchange ideas, and invent. Thanks to my colleagues in New Jersey TESOL for their support and encouragement.

Thanks to the many people who advised and encouraged me, and who read, field-tested, and commented on the manuscript in its early forms—especially Kari Noren and Dick Buehler.

I thank Loretta Lustig and Morissa Lipstein for the artwork that enlivens the reproducible pages; Rebecca Rauff for so carefully copyediting the manuscript and offering helpful suggestions regarding content and the organization of the material; David Corona Design for designing and laying out the pages; and production manager Anne Burkett for making it all happen.

Thanks to Dennis Ross and Thomas Williams, who made a Sunday house call to doctor my computer monitor.

Thanks to my treasured daughter-in-law and personal assistant, Nadine Simms, for creating the time for me to work on this Teacher's Kit by doing the zillion other things that needed to be done, from answering the mail to chopping vegetables.

Thanks, Mom. For the usual: Everything.

And finally to the people who taught me how to use the tools: the staff of Landmark Education Corporation, I thank you for the courses that inspire a vision of a world that works, a world in which nations communicate with words rather than with weapons of war.

A Word from the Author

In 1985, a friend of mine participated in a PTA and police search party that combed Queens, New York, all night through a torrential downpour, looking for a lost boy who had just arrived in the United States and could speak only five words of English. I was held spellbound with the drama and felt greatly relieved at its happy outcome. I, in turn, told the story to my ESL classes at School Two in Fort Lee, New Jersey.

The lost boy's story struck a nerve with my intermediate students; they were as wide-eyed as I had been, and suddenly the dams burst with a flood of their own stories and experiences. They had never spoken so much English! I sensed that my *beginning* students would also have a strong reaction to the story if I could only get it across to them. Having just arrived in the United States themselves, what had happened to the lost boy could easily happen to them. They were in dire need of the survival skills that the lost boy had not had time to learn.

I sketched 300 primitive line drawings to make the story comprehensible, wrote a sentence to go with each picture, and named the boy Taro. Since my students could not read English, I told the story orally. The students' emotional involvement with Taro seemed to magically glue new English words and sentences in their memories. With repeated listenings and activities based on the pictures, my preliterate students began to sight-read. This developed their confidence, and they were soon cracking the code of sound/symbol correspondences.

I found that advanced English-language learners, native English speakers, and adults also enjoyed the story; Taro's adventure served as a discussion starter for many different themes. Learners felt supported in expressing their own concerns and became aware that the dramas and emotional conflicts in their lives were stories worth telling, too. Taro's story provided much of the language students needed to share their experiences. *Where Is Taro?* was more than a story, it was a catharsis.

Some fictionalizing, many exacting choices in vocabulary and structure, expert editorial input from Dr. Marilyn Rosenthal at Harcourt Brace, and the clear, four-color illustrations by Loretta Lustig have brought the story to its present form as a picture novel. Linguistically economical and emotionally satisfying, it is appropriate for students of English throughout the world. Now, more even than a catharsis, *Where Is Taro?* has become the basis for a new kind of language program. I hope you and your students will enjoy this "novel approach" to learning English. This Teacher's Kit will launch you in your use of the novel, but don't stop there. Experiment and invent, and encourage your students to do likewise.

I am interested in your and your students' reactions to the story of Taro, and I will answer your class if you want to have a "write to the author" activity when your students finish reading the novel. Address class mail to me at my home address below, or in care of Harcourt Brace, Orlando, Florida.

Elizabeth Claire
302 Nedellec Drive
Saddle Brook, NJ 07662
U.S.A.

P.S. Teachers can help other students avoid Taro's traumatic experience! Help your students make I.D. cards on their first day of school and demonstrate that they are to carry the I.D. cards with them at all times. If possible, verify that every student knows the way home or will be picked up by a family member or friend on the first day of school.

About the *Where Is Taro?* Program

PROGRAM COMPONENTS

There are three components to the *Where Is Taro?* program:

- The Novel *(Where Is Taro?)*
- The Cassette
- The Teacher's Kit (a combined Teacher's Guide and Activity Book)

This section will familiarize you with the design and use of each component.

The Novel *(Where Is Taro?)*

Where Is Taro? is the first of a new genre—the "novel approach" to acquiring English. It is a basic whole-*second*-language textbook in disguise. Its goal is to build students' confidence and excitement about English by focusing their attention on Taro's story and their own experiences rather than on isolated elements of language.

Story Synopsis. Taro is a twelve-year-old boy who arrives in the United States from Japan with little English and a lot of worries about schoolwork and making friends.

On his first day in school, Taro attempts to communicate but fails. On the second day, sharing lunch helps him make some new friends, and he realizes that people can communicate in ways other than verbal language. However, following his new friends after school, he takes the wrong bus and gets lost. Taro has not yet learned his phone number or address, and he has left his I.D. card at home on the kitchen table. He knows only that he lives in "Ja-ku-son Hai-tsu." He attempts two times to ask for directions but a torrential downpour complicates things, forcing him to seek shelter under a stairway until the rain lets up. It is dark when he takes a bus going to Jackson Heights, and when he gets off at the landmark he is looking for, a big white gas station, it turns out to be the wrong one. A stranger offers to help, but Taro is wary because of his father's warning: "Don't talk to strangers."

Meanwhile Taro's parents, the police, and his classmates and their parents are out looking for him. Taro is cold, wet, hungry, and afraid, but he takes heart from a word of encouragement from his native language—*gambaro* (have courage, keep going)—and the philosophy, "It is not easy, but I can do it." Taro repeats this to himself as he faces each setback. Taro finally tries a public telephone, even though he can speak no English. He speaks frantically to the operator in his native language. A telephone operator who speaks Japanese is called in to help. Taro is able to read her the letters on a street sign; she notifies the police and links him to safety. The police take Taro to his school, where his worried parents and the search party have gathered. They cheer his arrival and provide warmth, hugs, food, and tea. His ordeal is over, and at the end he can proudly and meaningfully say, "It was not easy, but I did it."

Audience. The novel *Where Is Taro?* can be used with *students age seven and up*, at any English ability level, anyplace in the world. Students learning English as a foreign language can identify with Taro and his experiences just as easily as students living in the United States. Who among us hasn't been lost or feared being lost? All students can put themselves in Taro's place. Taro is not just a boy from Japan, he is Every Newcomer—male or female, child or adult, immigrant or visitor.

When used as a *core* whole-second-language text, *Where Is Taro?* is most appropriate for students in grades two to nine, in beginning and multilevel classes. The novel forms a bridge for crossing curriculum areas, and this Teacher's Kit contains many activities involving math, social studies, art, and self-expression.

For advanced and/or older students, the novel may be used as a springboard for conversation and writing, and for a first book report. It may be used as an introduction to literature with an analysis of character, setting, conflict, plot, climax, theme, and dramatic devices (such as foreshadowing, scene shifting, and suspense).

This Teacher's Kit provides suggestions for raising and lowering the difficulty level of the question banks and activities to meet your students' abilities. Using this guide, you will be able to challenge each of your classes and tailor activities to meet individual student's needs.

Language. Conversational, story-telling English is used throughout the novel. The sentences in the text are short, generally four to eight words long, and the language is natural: present, past (regular and irregular), and future verb tenses are used. Complex sentences, participles, and the passive voice occur rarely.

The novel's vocabulary base of 440 high-frequency words includes the terms most frequently taught to first-year students in these categories: family members, colors, numbers, food, time, weather, school subjects, classroom objects, body parts, clothing, transportation, descriptive adjectives, daily activities, action verbs, nationalities, and feelings. All words are presented in meaningful contexts.

First-year survival skills such as greeting people, identifying oneself, making introductions, making friends, using the telephone, describing people and places, asking for directions, and getting help in emergencies are woven into the story line.

Pictures. Three hundred full-color illustrations provide the all-important comprehensible input for each concept in the novel. These illustrations not only make the story understandable and easy to work with, they can be used to practice grammatical patterns and to teach hundreds of additional vocabulary items.

Themes and Values. This story of how a new arrival copes with loneliness, frustration, and trouble brings out a variety of literary themes and values. Taro has personal strengths and weaknesses, and his credo of "It is not easy, but I can do it" can inspire youngsters challenged by the difficulties of learning English. Taro's new friends are from many cultures, providing an opportunity to discuss and contrast different customs, foods, languages, expectations, and relationships. The story also contains the theme of similarity and relatedness—all people love their families and their children; all people need food, shelter, safety, friends, and kindness; all people face challenges, make mistakes, and have lessons to learn. Woven into the fabric of the novel are the principles of tolerance and cooperation among all races and language groups, and the appreciation of the fundamental value of each human being.

Organization. The novel has fifteen chapters, ranging from two to five pages each. Every chapter ends with a sign inviting the readers to "Stop and Talk." The picture panels are numbered to enable students to follow the story line easily and locate specific panels quickly.

The Cassette

This 35-minute cassette contains a dramatic reading of the novel by the author, with music and sound effects. The rate of speech is slightly slower than normal conversation, with short pauses between panels. There is no distortion of the rhythm or melody of conversational English. This careful pace allows beginning students to connect meaning, sound, and written symbols. Special music and the invitation to "Stop and Talk" mark the end of each chapter.

The cassette is designed for use with the *Where Is Taro?* novel. However, with more advanced students, the cassette can be used independently to practice listening and visualization skills.

The Teacher's Kit (Teacher's Guide and Activity Book)

The Teacher's Kit provides everything you need to fully exploit the learning opportunities embedded in the *Where Is Taro?* novel. In the guide section, you'll find general strategies for introducing the novel and pre-reading, reading, and post-reading activities for students at various stages of language acquisition. With this guide, you can tailor your teaching to each class and to each individual student, if need be.

The activity section is the heart of this guide. For each chapter, you'll find:

- a **Question Bank** consisting of multilevel comprehension questions, extension questions, and predictive questions. (Since the extension questions extend the story of Taro to the students' own lives, they are marked *ESL* for students who are learning English in the United States and *EFL* for students who are learning English as a foreign language in some other country.) The language level needed to answer each question is indicated by a system of + signs. (See page 6 for an explanation of the system.)

- illustrated **blackline master activity sheets** that contain listening, speaking, reading, writing, and self-expression experiences at four language ability levels.

Detailed instructions for using the activity sheets are also provided.

- a variety of **language development activities**, including Total Physical Response (TPR) activities, visualizations, culture sharing, research projects, survival skills, art projects, class trips, and creative writing.

In addition to the chapter-specific activities described above, the Teacher's Kit includes ideas for **culminating activities** to be used after students have completed the entire novel. An **appendix** contains two vocabulary lists, one showing the words in the order of their appearance in the novel and the other arranged alphabetically.

PROGRAM APPROACH AND THEORETICAL FOUNDATIONS

The *Where Is Taro?* program brings the "whole language" approach into the second-language classroom, incorporating listening, speaking, reading, writing, and survival skills in a literature-based curriculum. Beginning students are treated to a story whose narrative drive stimulates identification with the lead character and an interest in what becomes of him. Embedded in the story are the functional language structures students need to make friends, relate in games, talk about their feelings, and survive in their classrooms and on the street. Beginners can encounter the new language aurally at first, made comprehensible with the pictures and setting. An aural presentation can form the basis for learning vocabulary and intuiting grammar, and can be followed shortly by reading, speaking, and writing.

Acquisition vs. Learning

This "whole-second-language" approach combines the best of whole language with the best of today's second-language acquisition theories. Researcher Stephen Krashen's input hypothesis of language acquisition (*Second Language Acquisition and Second Language Learning*, Oxford: Pergamon, 1981) inspires the use of this approach. Krashen makes the distinction between the *acquisition* of language, exemplified by young children acquiring their mother tongue, and the *learning* of language, as in a traditional language class, where vocabulary is presented, grammar points are

explained and practiced, and students' attention is focused on the language itself.

The *Where Is Taro?* program allows for *acquisition* to take place first; the focus is on the story or on the students and their activities. You may choose (or not) to have your students *learn* the grammar rules *after* they have unconsciously internalized those rules.

The Four Stages of Acquisition

Krashen identifies four distinct stages of language acquisition: comprehension (preproduction), early production, speech emergence, and intermediate fluency. We all know that students don't fit neatly into these four stages or progress uniformly from one to the next. Nevertheless, the stages provide a useful framework for organizing teaching materials and techniques. Below is an overview of students' abilities and needs at each stage of acquisition, along with appropriate teaching strategies and examples from *Where Is Taro?*

Stage 1: Comprehension (Preproduction). Students at this stage of acquisition need opportunities to *listen* to comprehensible, authentic, engaging language. A student's "silent period" is an excellent language-learning strategy, not a problem that needs fixing. When students are not required to speak at this stage, more new language input can cross the affective filter and bind in their memories.

Although students at this stage may be silent, they can comfortably and successfully respond to a variety of tasks and directions. Teachers are encouraged to

- use Total Physical Response (TPR) activities (example: *Point to the plane.*)
- ask questions that focus on a concrete item or picture and can be answered by a simple yes or no, nodding or shaking of the head, or pointing (examples: *Is this a plane? Is this boy's name Bobby? Where's the taxi?*)
- demonstrate the meanings of new vocabulary items (for example, point when you say *point*)
- encourage group responses, to avoid putting pressure on individuals
- let individuals decide when they are ready to risk speaking, and support their efforts with encouragement and praise

This silent stage may end sooner on the playground and in ESL class than it does in more rigorous academic settings. Make sure that the students' mainstream teachers are also aware of ways to add comprehensible input to their aural presentations.

Stage 2: Early Production. In this stage, students are venturing one-word utterances or short phrases. Teachers should

- do more-complex TPR activities to increase vocabulary and aural comprehension of longer utterances
- ask questions that can be answered with one word
- ask questions that provide their own simple answer choices (examples: *Is the plane from Japan or Mexico? Is Taro a boy or a girl?*)
- offer more challenge by asking *WHo, WHat, WHere,* and *WHen* questions that require a one-word recall response (examples: *Where is the plane from? What is the boy's name? Who met them at the airport?*)
- ask questions that engage the students in higher-order thinking skills and conjecture (examples: *Who was on the plane? How many people are in Taro's family? Where are Taro's grandmother and grandfather?*)
- teach the phrase *I don't know*

Stage 3: Speech Emergence. At this stage students have a larger language base, have gained more confidence with language content and structures, and are able to risk longer phrases and complete sentences. This stage and the next one are characterized by native-language grammar pattern influences and native-language sound system interference, traditionally referred to as "errors." Research suggests, however, that these "mistakes" are actually valuable clues to the students' strategies for creating utterances in the new language. Teachers are advised to

- ask questions that require longer responses (phrases or sentences)
- ask questions that require recall rather than recognition of the answer (example: *Why was Taro happy?*)

- ask questions that involve combining information and producing longer discourse (example: *What were three things in New York City that surprised Taro and his mother and sister?*)

Stage 4: Intermediate Fluency. Students at this stage speak with some confidence and fluency on a variety of topics, but their language is still marked with native-language patterns and hesitations in word choice. They are ready to understand and respond to more linguistically complex questions. Teachers are encouraged to

- ask questions that require comparing, summarizing, analyzing, and hypothesizing (examples: *How was Taro's bed in the United States different from his bed in Japan? Tell the story of Taro's coming to the United States in your own words. Why do you think Taro's father came to Jackson Heights before Taro and his mother and sister did?*)
- focus on the *content* of students' responses rather than on their production errors
- use hand signals and facial expressions to help students learn self-monitoring. (For example, if you teach your students that when you point over your shoulder with your thumb, you are signaling the past tense, you can use this gesture to have a student self-correct after inappropriately using a present-tense verb. Likewise, you can hold up two fingers to help students remember to add an /s/ sound at the end of a plural word.) Don't overuse this strategy to the point of diminishing communication!

The Value of Reading

Language researcher Frank Smith says that reading for pleasure is the *most* efficient method of vocabulary building for school-age students. He points to research showing that a daily period of silent, sustained reading of self-selected materials produces better writers and spellers than a similar amount of time spent in teaching spelling and grammar (*Understanding Reading* [New York: Holt, Rinehart & Winston, 1982]). *Where Is Taro?* brings to ESL/EFL students these benefits as well as the fun of reading for pleasure.

Further support for a literature-based approach to language study is found in Goodman, 1986 (cited in Krause International Publications Staff, eds. *English as a Second Language Curriculum Resource Handbook* [New York: Krause Organization Limited, 1993], p. 21): "New language may be learned more easily by listening to and reading a well-illustrated story than by practicing a pattern such as the formation of the regular past tense." While students may need to practice some isolated units of language, those units that come from, and can be put back into, a meaningful context are most likely to be remembered and used.

Total Physical Response

James Asher's very popular and effective Total Physical Response (TPR) method inspired the TPR activities for each chapter *(Learning Another Language Through Actions* [Los Gatos, Ca: Sky Oaks Productions, 1977]). These activities create kinesthetic involvement, so the whole body associates and remembers actions in concert with verbal instructions.

The Affective Filter

Researchers and teachers have found that language acquisition occurs most rapidly in supportive environments, where students cooperate more than they compete with their classmates, where they experience enhanced self-esteem, and where they are empowered to direct some facets of their language learning. Stephen Krashen posits an *affective filter* through which language learning must take place. In "threatening" situations, students raise their protective defenses (affective filter), and language input is either not registered or quickly forgotten.

Speaking is the most complex of language performances, requiring an integration of sound, meaning, memory, grammar, and lip, tongue, and throat muscles. Error is inevitable; criticism or embarrassment is possible; and self-esteem is threatened. Krashen encourages teachers to lower the affective filter by taking the focus off production, allowing students to speak when they feel ready. This Teacher's Kit provides a variety of activities that will challenge your students while keeping the affective filter lowered.

PROGRAM OBJECTIVES

As a whole second language experience, *Where Is Taro?* may be used to meet a multitude of teacher and student objectives, depending on your students' ages, needs, and abilities. These include, but are not limited to, the following:

- Cognitive objectives: to enjoy a novel; to learn or sharpen survival skills; to develop listening comprehension; to develop reading comprehension; to learn to appreciate good literature; to learn new vocabulary; to learn to sight-read; to learn sound/symbol correspondences in context; to develop observation and thinking skills; to compare one's situation with Taro's; to expand speaking and writing skills; to become aware of the rhetorical devices in a novel.

- Affective objectives: to develop confidence; to function in an English-speaking environment; to express one's experiences and emotions; to imagine or recall the impressions, surprises, and concerns of one's first days in a new country; to enjoy cooperative activities with others.

- Interpersonal objectives: to listen to and speak with others; to learn to ask others for assistance; to learn of the network of family, school, and community support available to one; to share with others; to develop a concern for others; to empathize with others' difficulties; to learn ways of helping others; to become aware of similarities and differences in cultural behavior patterns; to learn to respect and value diversity; to write or perform for others.

Working with *Where Is Taro?*

GETTING READY

It's a good idea to become familiar with the novel before using it in the classroom. This won't take long. You can read the novel or preview the cassette in about 35 minutes. Then skim the Teaching Suggestions and Activity Sheets in this kit to see the range of materials available to you and your students.

Preparing for each day's lesson is quite simple. With the level and needs of your class in mind, decide

- how much of the novel you will read,
- which objectives you wish to meet, and
- which, if any, of the Activity Sheets and Extension Activities you will use.

Select a variety of teaching modes so you can match the different learning styles of your students. (Change modes *before* the students tire of an activity.) Collect any necessary realia for vocabulary instruction, and any materials you want to use for TPR activities. If you plan to use the cassette, make sure your tape player works. Finally, photocopy the Activity Sheets you plan to use.

MATCHING STRATEGIES TO STUDENTS AT THE FOUR STAGES OF LANGUAGE ACQUISITION

Where Is Taro? may be introduced to students at any stage in their language acquisition, including the very first week of instruction. Little prior experience with English is needed; ***Where Is Taro?* works even with preliterate students.**

At the same time, **no students are too advanced to read *Where Is Taro?*** for enjoyment and as an impetus for sharing feelings and experiences. Just select appropriate objectives and adjust the pace to fit the level(s) and needs of your class.

Where Is Taro? is particularly appropriate for use in multilevel classrooms. To assist you in matching students with appropriate activities, the questions and Activity Sheets in this Teacher's Kit are keyed to Stephen Krashen's four stages of language acquisition (see pages 3–4).

The questions in the Question Bank for each chapter are coded with plus (+) signs: + = Stage 1; ++ = Stage 2; +++ = Stage 3; ++++ = Stage 4. However, you can increase or decrease the difficulty of most questions in the Question Banks, using the strategies below.

To **decrease** the difficulty of a question, speak at a slightly slower-than-normal pace, repeat the question cheerfully, use gestures to illustrate meanings, and/or point to the panel or page that contains the answer. Use people's names rather than pronouns. If possible, break the question into simpler parts.

Examples:

1. Breaking down a Stage 2 Question for a Stage 1 Student: *Where did the taxi take them?*

   Point to the taxi. That's right. Point to Taro and his family. "Family" means mother, father, sister, and Taro. Did the taxi take Taro's family to Japan? (No.) Did the taxi take Taro's family to their new home? (Yes.) Where did the taxi take them? (New home.) Right!

2. Breaking down a Stage 3 Question for a Stage 2 Student: *Why did the bus driver stop the bus?*

   Point to the bus driver. Very good. Did the bus driver stop the bus? Mime stepping on a brake. *(Yes.) Did Taro get off the bus?* Mime fingers walking off a book, stepping down. *(Yes.) Why did the bus driver stop the bus? (Taro wanted to get off.)*

To **increase** the difficulty of a question, ask it with the students' books closed, with no visual cues, and/or at a normal speaking pace.

When the students have heard the basic question forms repeatedly, invite volunteers to be the leader and ask questions of the others, or allow the students to ask and answer questions in pairs. Provide some formal practice with question forms, and write samples on the blackboard.

Using *Where Is Taro?* with Students at Stages 1 and 2

Introducing the Novel. Hold up the novel, point to the cover, and say the title; write the title on the board and help the students read it. Teach the words *title* and *author*. Demonstrate the meaning of the question *Where is ____ ?* using people and objects in the classroom.

Point to and name (or elicit if possible) the people and objects on the cover of the book *(children, boys, girls, talking on the telephone).* Ask which child they think is Taro. *Is Taro a boy or a girl? Where do you think Taro is from?* Review or teach the names of countries, including your students' native countries.

Ask the students to open their books to page one. Have the students notice the numbers on the panels. Review the numbers 1–20 if necessary. Write the numbers 1.1, 1.2, and 1.3 on the board. Point to each element as you read: *one point one, one point two, one point three.*

The students will probably want to flip through the pages to look ahead and see what happens in the story. If you want to maintain the suspense of the story, and the effectiveness of asking prediction questions, consider using large paper clips to "lock" the chapters not yet read.

Pre-Reading Strategies. Before starting each chapter, review the previous chapter(s) with the students to build confidence and anticipation. Then have the students look at the pictures in the new chapter and guess what is happening. If you like, you can pre-teach key vocabulary items, using realia, pictures, and/or TPR activities.

Comprehension and Reading Procedures. Read a page or a chapter aloud as the students follow the story line through the pictures. (Since Chapter 1 introduces seventy different words, you might want to break it up into several lessons for students with little or no previous exposure to English.) As you read, point to the illustrations and use actions, gestures, and facial expressions to make as much of the vocabulary comprehensible as you can. Speak at a somewhat slower pace than normal. Pause after each panel so the students can associate the sounds with the correct illustrations, but don't aim for word-for-word comprehension.

Next, reread a page at a time and ask questions, panel by panel, to review the vocabulary and familiarize the students with question forms. At first, ask for responses from the group rather than putting individuals on the spot. Impress upon the students that even nonverbal responses such as pointing or nodding their heads are sufficient for success; be enthusiastic over any demonstration of comprehension.

Provide repeated listenings to enable students to sight-read, guess meaning from context, develop phonics awareness, become more confident with English sounds and grammatical patterns, and prepare for speaking. Choose any of the following methods:

- Read sentences from a page or a two-page spread at random, as the students listen. Ask them to identify the panel by pointing to it or raising their hands to tell the panel number. Repeat this activity until your least-able students can identify the panels when you speak at a normal conversational pace.
- Play the relevant section of the cassette. Have students listen with their books open, following the printed text.
- Play the relevant section of the cassette. Have the students listen with their books closed, visualizing the story.
- Read a section of the story aloud. Invite the students to read along with you when they feel ready.
- Have the students work in pairs, taking turns reading the panels in a chapter.
- Do an oral cloze activity: Reread the chapter aloud as the students listen with their books closed. Omit the last word, or another key word, from each sentence, allowing the students to fill it in chorally or individually. Examples: *The taxi took them to their new ____. (home) Tomorrow you will go to your new ____ (school), she said.*
- Have the students work in pairs to do a sentence strip activity. (See Activity Sheets 1c, 5c, 7c, and 15a.)
- Choose any of the other Activity Sheets that provide practice needed by the students.

Post-Reading Strategies. Use the language and situations in the story of Taro to bring out your students' own experiences and feelings. Encourage your students to draw, speak, and write about themselves and to listen to and comprehend their classmates.

Follow the lead of your students, comparing and contrasting their experiences with Taro's story. Choose from the numerous Extension Activities suggested for each chapter, bringing in other content areas, hands-on projects, field trips, class visitors, and so forth, as time and opportunity permit.

When the students have completed the entire novel, use one or more of the Culminating Activities on pages 43–44. These activities encourage students to use the language they have learned and offer recognition for their accomplishments.

Using *Where Is Taro?* with Students at Stages 3 and 4

Introducing the Novel. Ask the students if they can remember (or imagine) their first day in the United States (or another English-speaking country). What troubles did (might) they have?

Tell the students they are going to read a novel about a boy who got lost on his third day in the United States. Explain that a *novel* is a long story with many events and characters. Tell them that a novel is not a true story, and that the characters are imaginary, but that the novel *Where Is Taro?* is based on something that really happened. Ask if anyone in the class has ever been lost; if so, have those students tell about their experiences.

Ask the students to describe the children on the cover of the book. Ask them to guess how the children feel and what they are talking about. Have the students guess as much as they can about the children on the cover, including their ages, nationalities, grades, and relationships to Taro or each other. Write down the students' guesses on chart paper. Later, you can look to see which predictions were right.

Ask questions such as these: *What would you do if you got lost in the United States and you couldn't speak English? What problems do you think you might have? Do you have a special way of getting courage when you are in trouble? What do you say to yourself when things are difficult?* Some students may pray or rely on guardian angels, saints, and the like; others may have lucky charms, amulets, or sayings. Ask your students who they can call for help. Do they know their parents' work telephone numbers? Do they have neighbors they can count on?

To prepare students for writing book reports and their own books, point out the various sections of the book, including the title page, the copyright page, and the table of contents. Have

them read the dedication and invite their comments. Have them notice the acknowledgments. Explain that acknowledgments are a way of thanking people who have helped create a book.

Pre-Reading Strategies. Before starting each chapter, choose one or more of the following warm-up activities.

- Have the students give an oral summary of the previous chapters.
- Have the students make predictions about what will happen in the next part of the story. Later, have them compare their predictions with what actually happened in the story.
- Ask the students to tell about personal experiences that will be relevant in the next chapter.
- Use an advanced TPR or visualization activity.

Comprehension and Reading Procedures. Have the students listen to a chapter on the cassette with their eyes closed and visualize the story. Ask w*h* questions and other open-ended questions (including *how* and *why* questions) that require more than one-word responses. Naturally, students' pronunciation, sentence structure, and word choice won't be perfect, even when they know the right answer to a question. Acknowledge the factual correctness of an answer and, when possible, reword a student's utterance to provide a better model—without requiring the student to imitate it or even focus on it. Later, you can provide practice with the needed structures.

Example:

Teacher: *Could Taro sleep?*
Student 1: (Shakes head no.)
Teacher: *That's right. He could not sleep. Why not?*
Student 2: Worry.
Teacher: *Yes! He was worried. Why was he worried?*
Student 3: He no speak English. No have friend.
Teacher: *You're right. He had a good reason to worry, didn't he? He couldn't speak English, and he didn't have any friends. That's a serious problem. When you first started school here, did you worry?*

Student 4: Yeah.

Teacher: *What did you worry about?*

Student 4: Same like Taro. I no can speak English, no any friend.

Teacher: *That was a difficult time for you, wasn't it? Just like Taro, you didn't speak English and you didn't have any friends. Do you have friends now?*

Student 4: Yeah. Billy my friend.

Teacher: *That's great. Friends are important, aren't they?*

Next, have the students open their books and read the chapter silently. Invite students at stage 4 to analyze, summarize, discuss and debate, compare and contrast, and/or determine cause and effect. Have the students express their reactions and feelings about the events in the story. Connect the students' personal experiences with Taro's.

If you want the students to practice reading orally, have them work in pairs, reading alternating panels or pages. Circulate among the pairs, demonstrating expressive English intonation as needed. For additional speaking practice, have the students make up their own questions and check each other's comprehension of the story.

Note: Depending on your objectives and the students' abilities, you may wish to read more than one chapter at a time, or even assign the novel for homework over several days, and spend most of your class time on discussion, literary concerns, language extension, and personal sharing activities.

Post-Reading Strategies. Choose appropriate Extension Activities for each chapter, based on your students' level(s) and interests. Encourage the students to express their own feelings, opinions, and experiences in a variety of written and spoken formats.

When the students have completed the entire novel, use several of the Culminating Activities on pages 43–44 for additional creative language practice.

WORKING WITH THE ACTIVITY SHEETS

The forty-five reproducible Activity Sheets provide convenience and flexibility for busy teachers. There are two or more Activity Sheets for use with each chapter of *Where Is Taro?* Each Activity Sheet has multiple uses. You might make

enough copies of a sheet to do a listening activity one day and a reading and writing or speaking activity the next day. Suggestions and guidelines for using each Activity Sheet are provided in the Questions and Activities section, beginning on page 14. The guidelines indicate which Activity Sheets are appropriate for students at each of the four stages of language acquisition. In addition, the following icons are used to indicate activity types:

 listening activity

 reading activity

 speaking activity

 writing activity

 art activity

 self-expression activity

game

Use the following suggestions to increase or decrease the difficulty level of any activity.

Listening activities

To *decrease* difficulty:

- Speak slowly.
- Repeat several times.
- Give visual clues.
- Clarify answers immediately.
- Have the students self-check.

To *increase* difficulty:

- Speak at a normal rate.
- Let the students know that you will say each item only once.
- Go through the entire activity before giving feedback.
- Use a more linguistically challenging set of questions.
- Change the activity to a speaking or writing activity that requires the students to generate the language.

Reading activities

To *decrease* difficulty:

- Read the items or the selection to the students.
- Have the students read to each other.

To *increase* difficulty:

- Cover the pictures and other visual clues before photocopying the activity.

Speaking activities

To *decrease* difficulty:

- Don't pressure students to speak when they are not ready.
- Don't call attention to a student's speech errors. Give positive feedback and encouragement.
- Allow students to refer to the text or use pictures and props when speaking.
- Model the words or sentences for the students.
- Have students speak to a partner rather than in front of the class.

To *increase* difficulty:

- Have individual students generate the language with their books closed and no cues.

Writing activities

To *decrease* difficulty:

- Do the activity as a class: Write the elicited answers on the blackboard or have student volunteers write them. Have the students copy the correct answers.
- Have the students work in pairs or small groups.
- Dictate the selection to the students so they can hear the missing words.
- Allow the students to consult or copy from *Where Is Taro?*
- Allow the students to use a bilingual dictionary.

To *increase* difficulty:

- Cover the word bank before photocopying a page.
- Have the students write from dictation without any visual clues.
- After the students complete the activity, have them rewrite the selection in their own words on another sheet of paper.

WORKING WITH THE EXTENSION ACTIVITIES

The Questions and Activities section beginning on page 14 contains chapter-by-chapter suggestions for a wide variety of language development and enrichment activities. Choose the themes and teaching modes that best meet the needs of your students. In addition to those chapter-specific activities, the following general activity types may be used with any chapter in the novel.

Total Physical Response (Action Drills)

Objectives: To review action verbs from the story and learn additional verbs in the simple (command) form; to develop listening skills; to associate sound with meaning kinesthetically.

Procedure: Have the students listen, watch, and imitate your actions as you give commands and act them out. (They should not say the commands after you.) Repeat and model each command several times. Then give the commands without modeling the actions and have the students perform the actions, praising them enthusiastically when they do. Conduct the TPR at a lively pace so that students are successful but not bored. Let there be no negative consequences for mistakes. In small classes, everyone can participate at once. In larger classes, have groups take turns following your commands while the other students listen and watch. As the students become confident, they can volunteer to perform individually or to give the commands to others.

Visualization

Objectives: To increase listening comprehension; to engage the imagination.

Procedure: Have the students close their eyes and visualize themselves in a scene as you describe it. You can leave the visualization open-ended by not giving a conclusion; have the students talk in pairs about how to complete the scene. Or have the students write about the scene they visualized, using the first person and the past tense.

Copying Text

Objectives: To engage the kinesthetic learning mode; to become familiar with spelling and letter formation.

Procedure: Have the students copy a page or a chapter of the story once they are familiar with its meaning and can sight-read or decode it successfully. Have them check each other's work for accuracy. For students new to the Roman alphabet, provide guidance in letter formation. Point out the difference between a printed letter *a* and the book letter *a*. (The book typeface is otherwise very similar to the printing style taught in most U.S. schools.)

Dictated Written Cloze

Objective: To correlate listening, reading, and writing, engaging three learning modes.

Procedure: Use a section of the novel to create your own cloze activity. Delete words at regular intervals (often, every seventh word) or select particular words (e.g., prepositions) to delete. Distribute copies of the text with blanks for the deleted words. Have the students write in the missing words as you read the entire selection.

Written Cloze

Objectives: To practice reading or recall; to improve spelling.

Procedure: Create a cloze activity as described above. List the deleted words in a word bank at the bottom of the page. Have the students choose words from the word bank to complete the text. (This activity can be made more difficult by not providing a word bank or by covering the word bank before duplicating the page.)

Dictation

Objectives: To transfer what is heard to written language; to practice conventions of spelling, punctuation, and capitalization.

Procedure: Have the students write several sentences from the story as you dictate them.

Creating a Picture Dictionary

Objectives: To review vocabulary; to practice spelling; to engage the kinesthetic learning mode; to build self-esteem.

Procedure: Demonstrate how to fold a piece of unlined paper in half lengthwise twice, then width-wise twice. When opened, the paper will be divided into sixteen sections. In each section, have the students write a word from the story and illustrate it. (See example below.) You might also have the students include additional words they have learned through relating their own experiences to Taro's. Have the students use only one side of the paper.

 Note: Most verbs in the story are used in the past tense. Teach the present tense as well, and have the students write both forms in the same section.

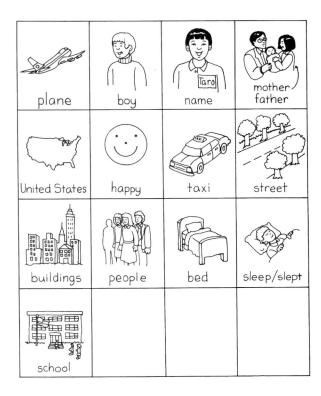

Sharing Culture

These are group discussions on cultural or language topics sparked by the novel. Specific suggestions are given with each chapter.

Sharing Experiences (Interviewing)

Objectives: To practice speaking English; to create relationships by sharing personal experiences; to practice writing and editing skills.

Procedure: Have the students work in pairs or small groups. Create and duplicate a list of questions that connect Taro's experience with your students' own experiences. Use appropriate questions from the Question Banks and add your own. Have student A interview student B and take notes; then they switch roles. Encourage the students to ask additional questions or talk together about anything interesting that they learn. Then have the students write "news stories" about their partners.

Have them read their stories aloud in small groups. The other group members listen, ask questions to clarify their understanding and to get more information, and offer suggestions for improving clarity, grammar, word choice, vividness of detail, and so on.

Doing Research

Objectives: To practice research skills; to engage in cooperative learning; to practice giving oral reports.

Procedure: Divide the students into small groups and give each group several information questions to research. (Choose questions based on issues suggested by the novel.) Have the students use a variety of sources such as maps, almanacs, encyclopedias, people in the school, and community workers. After completing their research, the group members should choose a speaker to report the results to the class.

Taking a Survey

Objectives: To learn to conduct research; to practice question forms; to collect information.

Procedure: Prepare and distribute a survey form such as the one below:

Survey	
Title: _____	
Question: _____	
Name	Answer
1. _____	
2. _____	
3. _____	
4. _____	
5. _____	
6. _____	
7. _____	
8. _____	
9. _____	
10. _____	
11. _____	
12. _____	
13. _____	
14. _____	
15. _____	

Have the students choose a question and write a title for the survey. Then have them ask fifteen people the same question, recording each person's name and response. Finally, have the students write a sentence about each person on another sheet of paper.

Creating Bar Graphs

Objectives: To report survey results; to learn how to represent data visually.

Procedure: Prepare and distribute a bar graph form following this sample:

| Title: _____ |
| Question: _____ |

Category	Number of People														
	1	2	3	4	5	6	7	8	9	10	11	12	13	14	15
_____															
_____															
_____															
_____															
_____															
_____															
_____															
_____															
_____															

Have the students work in pairs or small groups to fill in the title and question for the bar graph and label the categories based on their survey responses. Then have the students enter the results of their surveys, shading in the squares to make a bar graph. On another sheet of paper, have them write sentences based on the bar graph. (Example: *Five people are from Mexico. One person is from Italy.*) Have a group spokesperson explain the bar graph to the class or to another small group.

Discovering Grammar

Teaching grammar *after* language has been acquired can generate the "aha!" experience that makes learning very satisfying. The novel's simple but natural language patterns assist the students in making unconscious generalizations about grammar. After the students are familiar with the story, you can use examples from the text to illustrate various grammatical terms and rules.

EVALUATING STUDENTS' WRITTEN WORK

The best method of correction is motivated self-correction. For most activities, it is more efficient to have students compare their answers with a peer than for you to collect and correct them. Have the students volunteer answers for you to write on the blackboard as they check their own or their partner's paper. Let the students score their own papers. Collect the papers to spot-check how well students are editing their work; return them for students to use again for additional language practice. Give positive verbal feedback to the class and to individuals to be sure the students are acknowledged for their work.

Students learning English need a great deal of writing practice, but you need not collect and correct every piece of writing your students do. Students generally do not learn from red marks on papers anyway, but from interacting with a reader. Have the students read each other's writings in pairs or small groups. Demonstrate how to read and comment in a supportive way, how to take interest in each other's writings, and how to ask questions to clarify meaning. Ask the students to discuss spelling, punctuation, and grammar suggestions that might improve their partner's writing. Circulate to monitor the process, give encouragement, and offer suggestions for improvement.

More-advanced students can refine their skills by becoming "editors" and "consultants" for the beginning student in a multilevel class. Consider inviting some native-English speakers from mainstream classes to serve as guest readers/editors from time to time. If you give these peer teachers some guidance and support, the interactions can be very productive.

Maintain a portfolio (a folder of written work and comments) for each student as a record of his or her progress. Have students select their best work (pieces that have been peer-edited and then rewritten) to post in the classroom for others' enjoyment and/or to include in their portfolio. Schedule conferences with each student several times a year. Point out the growth in each one's abilities, and avoid making comparisons with other students' rates of progress.

Multilevel Question Banks and Activities

Note: In the procedures for the Activity Sheets, the following icons are used:

 listening   reading   speaking   writing   art   self-expression   game

CHAPTER 1: TARO COMES TO THE U.S.

Question Bank

Eighty questions are developed below for Chapter 1, to demonstrate how you can provide opportunities for success for students at stages 1 and 2 as well as students who already speak some English. Subsequent chapters will not include the "easier" questions, which you can easily invent as needed. Some suggested answers are given. Other answers are possible. The plus signs (+) indicate the appropriate stage of acquisition for each question (+ = stage 1; ++++ = stage 4).

+ Point to the plane.

++ Where's the plane from? (Japan)

++ Where is it going? (the United States)

+ Point to the boy.

++ What's the boy's name? (Taro)

++ What's your name?

++ Where is Taro from? (Japan)

++ Where are you from?

+++ What is Taro doing? (He's looking out the window. He's sitting on a plane. He's flying to the U.S.)

+ Point to Taro's mother.

+++ What is she doing? (She's reading a magazine.)

+ Point to Taro's sister.

+++ What is she doing? (She's sleeping.)

++ Who was on the plane with Taro? (his mother and sister)

+++ Does Taro have a brother? (Teach "I don't know.")

+ Do you have any brothers?

+ Do you have any sisters?

+ (ESL) Did you come to the U.S. on a plane?

++ (ESL) Who was on the plane with you?

+ (EFL) Were you ever on a plane?

++ (EFL) Where did you go?

++ (EFL) Who went with you?

+++ (EFL) What did you do on the plane?

++ Who met Taro at the airport? (his father)

+ Point to Taro's father.

+++ How did Taro feel when he saw his father? (He was happy.)

++ (ESL) Who met you at the airport?

+++ (ESL) How did you feel when you came to the United States?

++ (ESL) Did you come to an airport in New York City (or ____)?

+ (EFL) Do you want to go to the United States?

++ (EFL) Who do you want to go with?

++ What is Taro's sister's name? (Yoko)

++ What is Taro's last name? (Yamada)

++ What is your last name? (Demonstrate meaning of *last name* as family name.)

++ Did Taro's family get into a taxi or on a bus? (into a taxi)

+ Point to the taxi.

++ Does Mr. Yamada have a car? (I don't know. Maybe not.)

++ Does your family have a car?

++ Where did the taxi take them? (to their new home)

++ (ESL) Did you go to your new home in a taxi, a bus, or a car?

++++ (ESL) What kinds of transportation did you use when you came to your new home in the United States?

++ (EFL) Did you ever move to a new home?

+++ (EFL) How did you travel to your new home?

++++ Why do you think Taro's family came to the United States?

14

++++ (ESL) Why did your family come to the U.S.?

++ (ESL) Did everyone in your family come to the U.S. at the same time?

++ (ESL) Did someone in your family come to the U.S. first to find a job and a home?

+++ (EFL) Will you ever go to the United States?

++ (EFL) Who in your family do you think will go with you?

++ Did Taro's family speak Japanese or English? (Japanese)

++ What language do you speak with your family?

++ What city are the Yamadas in? (New York)

++ What city do you live in?

++ Who said, "The streets are so wide"? (Mrs. Yamada)

+ Point to the street.

++ Are there wide streets in your city?

++ Is our school on a wide street or a narrow street?

++ Who said, "The buildings are so tall"? (Yoko)

+ Point to the tall buildings.

++ Are the buildings tall in your city?

++ Who said, "There are so many different people"? (Taro)

+ Point to the people.

+++ What things surprised Taro and his mother and sister?

+++ (ESL) What surprised you when you came to the United States?

++++ (EFL) What would surprise Taro if he came to this country?

++ Where will Taro live? (in Jackson Heights)

+ Is it easy for Taro to say *Jackson Heights*? (no)

++ In the United States, will Taro sleep in a bed or on a sofa? (in a bed)

+ Point to the bed.

++ In Japan, did Taro sleep in a bed or on a futon? (on a futon)

+ Point to the futon.

+ Do you sleep in a bed?

+++ What was different in Taro's new home? (the beds)

++++ (ESL) What was different about your new home?

++ When will Taro go to school? (tomorrow) (Use a calendar to clarify the meaning of *tomorrow*.)

++++ Do you think Taro should rest a few days before he goes to his new school?

++++ (ESL) How soon did you go to school after coming to this country?

++++ (EFL) If you moved to a new country, how many days would you wait before going to school?

++++ (ESL) What was the most exciting/worst/best thing about your trip to the United States?

Predictive Questions for Chapter 2:

+ Can Taro speak English?

+++ How much English do you think he knows?

+ Do you think Taro is very tired?

+ Will he sleep?

++ Do you think Taro will worry? (Use gestures and facial expressions to illustrate *worry*.)

++++ What do you think Taro will worry about?

Activity Sheets

1a. Listen and Circle (Stages 1–4)

• Have the students circle the letter of the picture that shows what you are saying.

1. *This is Taro's mother.* (b)
2. *A plane came to the United States.* (a)
3. *Taro was happy to see his father.* (c)
4. *They spoke in Japanese.* (d)
5. *In Japan, Taro slept on a futon.* (b)
6. *"Good night," said Taro.* (d)

• Write the above sentences on the blackboard. Have the students read the sentences silently and circle the correct pictures to demonstrate reading comprehension.

- Have the students work in pairs to play a game. Student A makes a statement about one of the pictures on the page; student B points to the correct picture. If student B is correct, he or she makes a statement about a different picture. If student B is mistaken, student A repeats the sentence and points to the correct picture, then takes another turn.

- Have the students write a sentence about each picture and compare their sentences with a partner.

1b. What Do You See? (Stages 1–4)

- Have the students point to the people and objects in the picture: *Taro, Taro's mother, Taro's father, Taro's sister, Taro's new home, the taxi, the street, the plane.*
- Call out sentences that tell what is happening and have the students point to the appropriate places in the picture. For example: *Mr. Yamada has a key. He is opening the door. Yoko is carrying her doll. The taxi is driving away. Mrs. Yamada is walking behind Taro,* and so forth.
- Use the picture to teach language structures and patterns such as past and future verbs forms, prepositions (*in front of, behind, between*) and ordinals (*first, second, third, fourth, last*). Have students point to pictures that show: *Who is going to open the door? Who was first up the stairs? Who will be last? Who is walking behind Yoko? Who is between Taro and Mr. Yamada?*

- Have the students read the words listed under the picture, locate each item, and write the letter of the item on the line.

  Answers: 1. E, 2. D, 3. G, 4. F, 5. C, 6. A, 7. H, 8. B

- Have the students name as many items as they can identify in the picture.

  Ask the students questions about what each person in the picture is doing, what they are carrying, where they are going, and so forth. For example: *What is Yoko carrying? What do you think is in the suitcases?*
- Ask questions to elicit extended discourse using the past and future tenses, such as *What just happened?* (The taxi stopped in front of their home; they got out of the taxi; Mr. Yamada paid the taxi driver) and *What is going to happen next?* (They are going to go into their home; they are going to eat/sleep/change their clothes).

- Have the students work in pairs to write as many words or sentences as they can to tell what they see in the picture.
- Write questions on the blackboard; have the students read the questions and write answers based on the picture.

- Have the students draw pictures showing their families going to their homes.
- Have the students talk in small groups about their pictures.
- Have the students write paragraphs about their pictures.
- Combine the pictures and paragraphs into a class magazine or anthology, or post them in the hall for other students to see.

1c. What Happened First? (Stages 1–4)

- Have the students cut the page into sentence strips. Have them mix the strips and then, working alone, arrange them in order to tell the story. Then have pairs of students compare their stories.

Answers:

1. One day, a plane left Japan and came to the United States.
2. Mrs. Yamada was on the plane with Taro and Yoko.
3. Mr. Yamada came to the airport to meet them.
4. The children were happy to see their father.
5. The family got into a taxi.
6. The taxi took them to their new home.

- Cut the page into sentence strips. Have the students work in pairs. Give each person three sentence strips. Have the partners read their sentences to each other without showing them, and decide the order of the sentences.

- Have the students cut the page into sentence strips and also cut on the solid, vertical lines to separate the pictures from the text. Have them play concentration in pairs or small groups, matching the sentences with the correct pictures.

- Have the students arrange the pictures in the correct order and tell or write the story in their own words.

1d. Tell a Story (Stages 1–4)

- Have the students complete the sentences, using the picture clues in each box.

- Have the students illustrate their stories.

- Show the students how to continue their stories on additional pages by folding sheets of paper into four panels.

- Have the students write and illustrate stories about their own real or imaginary moves to a new country, using sheets of paper folded into four panels.

1e. Interview a Partner (Stages 3, 4)

- Have partners interview each other about their trips to a new country. Tell students who have not moved to a new country to use their imaginations to create answers.

- Have each student write a story about a real or imaginary move, using the questions as a guide for details they can include.

Extension Activities

Total Physical Response Activity. Before class, sketch these items on separate pieces of paper: a plane, a bed, a house, a taxi, a tall building, a boy, and a girl. Post them in widely separated parts of the room.

In class, give the following TPR commands: *Point to the plane; point to the tall building; point to the bed; point to the taxi; point to the house; point to the boy; point to the girl; look at the tall building; look at the bed; look at the house; look at the girl; look at the taxi; look at the boy.* Limit the following commands to five or six students: *Go to the tall building; go to the house; go to the plane; go to the bed; go to the boy; go to the taxi; go to the girl.* Then mix the commands: *Point to the tall building; go to the house; look at the girl; go to the taxi; look at the bed; point to the boy; go to the tall building.*

TPR and Visualization: Traveling by Plane.

1. Sketch an airplane on the blackboard. Sit on a chair and place your arms on imaginary armrests. Have the students follow the commands as you say and model them. When the students are familiar with the TPR, invite them to close their eyes and visualize the activity.

   Say and model the following: *You are on an airplane: Fasten your seat belt. Look out the window. The plane is coming to the airport. The plane is landing. It stopped. Unfasten your seat belt. Stand up. Watch your head. Get your bag. Walk* (model walking in place) *to the front of the plane. Say thank you to the flight attendant. Say good-bye to the pilot. Walk off the plane. Walk and walk and walk. Look!* (point) *There's your family. They are meeting you at the airport. Run to them.* (run in place) *Hug your mother. Hug your grandmother.*

2. Draw a picture on the blackboard of suitcases on a conveyor belt as at an airport. Give and model the following TPR commands: *Go to the baggage claim area. Get your suitcases. Carry them. They are very heavy! Go out the door. Wait for a taxi. Here is a taxi. Put your suitcases in the trunk. Get in the taxi. Sit down. Tell the taxi driver where to go: 555 Anderson Street, please. Look out the window. Point to the tall buildings. Here is your new home. Get out of the taxi. Pay the driver. Walk up the stairs to your house. Take out your key. Open the door. Look at your new home. Go into the bedroom. Look at your bed. You're very tired. Put your head on the pillow. Close your eyes. Go to sleep.*

Family Members. Have the students bring in photographs or draw pictures of their families. Show a photo of your family, naming the people and their relationships to you. Then have individuals explain who the people in their pictures are. Provide vocabulary as needed: *family, grandmother, grandfather, grandparents, parents, uncle, aunt, cousin, brother, sister, son, daughter,* etc. Model questions for other students to ask: *Who is this? How old is he/she? Where does he/she live?* Have the students tell what country each family member lives in. Then have each student make a family album, drawing or pasting in pictures of family members on each page and writing several sentences about each picture (e.g., *This is my mother. Her name is _____. She speaks _____.*).

Discovering Grammar. The novel uses the past forms of verbs, except when people are speaking or thinking. The TPR activities use the basic form. Point out that verbs have different forms to show time. Make a chart of the verbs in Chapter 1, showing the form in which they appear in the novel (past form) and the form students will find in their dictionaries (basic form).

Transportation. Present pictures of several kinds of transportation: plane, bus, taxi, ship, bicycle, truck, car, and so on. Then have the students draw and label the different kinds of transportation they used (or would use) during their trip to the United States. Ask what transportation they use to come to school.

Geography and Map Study. Have ESL students locate their native countries on a globe and find the shortest air route from each one to your city. Have them name the major countries, states, bodies of water, islands, and other landmarks a plane would fly over. Have them use the map key to determine the air mileage, then make a bar graph to show the distance traveled by each member of the class.

In EFL classes, teach the names of your country's neighbors and major trading partners. Have the students locate each one on the globe and find the air routes from major cities to your city.

Doing Research. Have groups of students find the answers to the following questions and report the information they learned to the class. (Suggested resources are shown in parentheses.)

1. How far is it from Tokyo, Japan, to New York City? (globe, almanac)

2. What routes can a plane take from Japan to New York? (globe, airline or travel brochure)

3. How many hours does it take to fly from Tokyo to New York? (airline or travel brochure, the students' experience)

4. How fast does a jet fly? (encyclopedia, airline or travel agency)

5. What international airport is in New York City? (map)

6. How far is it from your home city to New York City?

7. How many hours would it take to fly from your home city to New York City?

8. What is the population of New York City? (almanac, atlas)

9. What is the population of Tokyo? (almanac, atlas)

10. What is the population of the largest city in your native country? (almanac, atlas)

11. Find Jackson Heights on a map of New York City. (NYC map)

First Experiences in the U.S. Pair the students. Have the partners take turns describing one of their first experiences in the U.S. If appropriate, have the students draw pictures to aid in their descriptions. Then have each student tell the class (or another pair) about his or her partner's experience. Encourage the students to ask questions and take an interest in each other's experiences. (Let EFL students imagine what might happen to them upon arriving in the U.S.)

Sharing Culture: First Impressions. Make a class list of cultural differences that seem obvious upon arriving in a different country (food, language, gestures, money, uses of transportation, types of home, etc.). Discuss how important these cultural difference are to new arrivals. How important are they after a long period of time? What similarities do your students see between cultures? Are the differences or the similarities more important? Why?

CHAPTER 2: TARO WORRIES

Question Bank

Ask Stage 1 and Stage 2 questions as needed, in addition to the following questions.

  ++ Could Taro sleep? (no)

 +++ Why not? (He was worried.)

  ++ (ESL) Could you speak English before you came here?

  ++ (ESL) Were you worried about going to school here?

  ++ (EFL) Do you think you could learn in an American school?

  ++ What does Taro say to feel better? (*Gambaro.* It is not easy, but I can do it.)

  ++ Is *gambaro* an English word or a Japanese word? (a Japanese word)

  + Do you know the alphabet in English?

  + Can you count in English—one, two, three . . . ?

 +++ (ESL) How much English did you know when you came here?

  ++ Can you read English?

Predictive Questions for Chapter 3:

 +++ Do you think Taro will go to the same school as his sister?

 +++ How do you think Taro will get to school?

  ++ Who do you think will go with him?

  ++ What grade do you think Taro is in?

  ++ Do you think Taro will understand anyone at school?

Activity Sheets

2a. Listen and Circle (Stages 1–4)

- Have the students circle the letter of the picture that shows what you are saying.
  1. *Taro could not sleep. He was worried.* (c)
  2. *In Japan, Taro had many friends.* (a)
  3. *Taro knew the letters of the alphabet.* (b)
  4. *Eleven.* (or: *Five and six are ____.*) (b)
  5. *E.* (or: *This letter comes after D.*) (a)
  6. *Taro fell asleep.* (a)

- Have the students work in pairs. Student A makes a statement about one of the pictures on the page; student B listens and points to the correct picture. If student B is correct, he or she makes a statement about a different picture. If student B is mistaken, student A repeats the sentence and points to the correct picture, then takes another turn. See additional suggestions provided for Activity Sheet 1a on pages 15–16.

2b. Complete the Sentences (Stages 1, 2)

- Have the students read the sentences and write the word for each picture clue. (Remember that in this type of activity, you can increase the difficulty level by covering the word bank before duplicating the page, or decrease the difficulty level by dictating the words that the students will write.)

Answers:

1. sleep, 2. friends, 3. speak, 4. I,
5. alphabet, 6. numbers

2c. What Worried You? (Stages 1–4)

- Elicit from your students the things that Taro was worried about and write them on the board. Have the students add any details they like. Have them read the story from the board. Elicit things that they worried about when they first came to the United States, or when they first started school. (In EFL classes, have the students imagine moving to another country and tell what they think they would worry about.)

- Have the students write their fears or draw pictures of them in the thought balloons. Have them draw their own faces.

- Have the students discuss their pictures with a partner.

Extension Activities

Total Physical Response: Going to Bed. Say and model commands such as these for students to follow: *You are getting ready for bed. Wash your face. Wash your hands. Brush your teeth. Put on your pajamas. Walk to your bed. Pull down the blanket. Pat the pillow. Climb into bed. Lie down. Put your head on the pillow. Pull up the blanket. Close your eyes. Open your eyes. You can't sleep. Worry. Worry. Worry.* (Demonstrate by biting fingernails, making faces, etc.) *Say* "Gambaro." *Count to twenty. Sing the alphabet song. Stop worrying. Close your eyes. Go to sleep.*

Discovering Grammar. Point out that when we talk about more than one thing, we use the plural form of a noun, which usually ends in *s*. Make a chart showing the singular and plural forms of nouns from Chapters 1 and 2.

Persistence. Talk about the Japanese word *gambaro* (gahm bah roh), which means "do my best" or "keep at it." *Gambate* (gahm bah tay) is the form used when speaking to another person. The expression is used to urge people on through fear and hardship for the sake of the group. Ask the students what expressions in their native languages help people through difficult times. Have the students create posters of encouraging words in their native languages to hang around the room. Whenever the students are frustrated, encourage them with words from their native languages or remind them, "It is not easy, but you can do it." Teach other American English expressions, such as "Keep your chin up" and "I think I can, I think I can, I think I can."

Feelings and Concerns of New Arrivals. Ask ESL students to recall and share the concerns and feelings they had upon arriving in the U.S. Ask what helped them, who helped them, and how they helped themselves. Have EFL students recall and discuss their first day of school. Ask how old they were, who came with them, what they were thinking and feeling, and what happened.

Abilities in English: Numbers.

1. Have the students count by ones, twos, fives, tens, and threes.

2. Send five or six students to the blackboard while the other students write at their seats. Dictate numbers at a pace that stretches the students but does not confuse or frustrate them.

3. Have the students practice reading numbers from the board.

4. Have the students practice saying and writing their addresses and telephone numbers.

Abilities in English: The Alphabet. Have the students recite the alphabet, identify letters, and practice writing letters. Then have the students recall and tell about the first words they learned in English.

Sharing Culture. If you have students from various language backgrounds, let them take turns teaching the rest of the class to count to five and say Taro's five words *(hello, goodbye, yes, no,* and *thank you)* in each language. (In an EFL classroom, have students share words and numbers from any other languages they know.)

Doing Research. Ask groups of students to find and report the answers to questions such as these:

1. When it is ten o'clock at night in New York City, what time is it in Tokyo? in your city? in your native country?

2. How many time zones are there in the United States? in your native country? in the world?

3. What is *jet lag*? Do you think Taro had jet lag?

CHAPTER 3: THE FIRST MORNING IN SCHOOL

Question Bank

Ask Stage 1 and Stage 2 questions as needed, in addition to the following questions.

++ What grade was Taro in? (seventh)

+++ What were three problems Taro had in school? (He couldn't read the books, he couldn't understand the teacher, and he felt sick.)

+ Does Taro understand the teacher? (no)

++ How did Taro feel all morning? (sick)

++++ What happened at lunchtime? (A boy spoke to Taro.)

++ Who was the first person to talk to Taro? (Ramón)

++++ Why do you think Ramón spoke to Taro?

++ Do you talk to new students when they come to this school?

+++ What problems did you have on your first days of school?

++ Who was the first person in this school to talk to you?

Predictive Questions for Chapter 4:

++++ What will happen in the afternoon?

++ Will Taro's father come to school to get him?

++++ What will Taro's parents do to help him?

Activity Sheets

3a. Listen and Circle (Stages 1–4)

• Have the students circle the letter of the picture that shows what you are saying.

  1. *Mr. Yamada went with Taro to his new school. They went by bus.* (d)

2. *Taro was in junior high school. He was in the seventh grade.* (c)

3. *Taro could not read the books.* (b)

4. *"Hi, my name is Ramón Soto," said the boy.* (a)

5. *"This is Jae Han Kim," said Lee. "She's from Korea."* (c)

6. *The bell rang. Lunchtime was over.* (d)

See additional suggestions provided for Activity Sheet 1a on pages 15–16.

3b. What Do You See? (Stages 1–4)

• Have the students point to the people and objects in the picture as you call out the words in random order.

• Have the students read the words, find each object in the picture, and write the correct letter next to each word.

Answers:

1. E, 2. B, 3. G, 4. F, 5. D, 6. I, 7. A, 8. C, 9. H

• Have the students name as many items as they can identify in the picture.

• Ask the students what each person in the picture is doing, where he or she is sitting, what is on his or her desk, and so forth.

• Have the students work in pairs to write as many sentences as they can to tell what they see in the picture.

• Have the students draw pictures showing themselves in your classroom or in a former classroom.

• Have the students talk about their pictures with a partner, and then write about their pictures.

• Have the students read each other's stories.

3c. What Are They Saying? (Stages 1–4)

- Have the students read the sentences in the first speech balloon. Have them follow the same sentence patterns to write what the other children are saying. Have them guess where Ramón and Susan might be from.

  Answers:
  1. I'm Lee Wong. I'm from China.
  2. I'm Jae Han Kim. I'm from Korea.
  3. I'm Ramón Soto. I'm from _____ .
  4. I'm Susan Bradley. I'm from _____ .
  5. I'm (student's name). I'm from _____ .

- Have the students make up and write a variety of things the children might say.

- Have the students draw their own faces and write two sentences that they would say.

Extension Activities

Visualization and TPR: Going to the Lunchroom. Say and model the following: *You are hungry. Take your lunch box to the lunchroom. Sit down next to a friend. Smile and say hi. Open your lunch box. You have a delicious lunch today! Unwrap your sandwich. Take a bite. Put a straw in your milk container. Drink some milk. Ahhh.*

Discovering Grammar. Demonstrate how to form negative sentences, using sample sentences from the first three chapters. Make a chart of corresponding affirmative and negative sentences.

Greetings and Introductions. Have the students practice greetings, farewells, and making introductions. Demonstrate a firm American handshake with each student. (In many cultures, people offer their hands very gently—but in the U.S., a firm handshake makes a better impression.)

School Locations. Take your students on a walk around the school. Point out and name various classrooms, the art and music rooms, the principal's and nurse's offices, the library, the lunchroom, the gym, and so on.

School Grades and Divisions. Teach or review ordinal numbers and the forms "grade five" and "fifth grade." Talk about the usual school divisions in the United States: elementary school (kindergarten to fifth or sixth grade), middle school or junior high school (sixth or seventh to eighth or ninth grade), high school (ninth or tenth through twelfth grade), and college or university.

Sharing Cultures. Ask students to tell about schools in their native countries. Teach the English names of school subjects so the students may describe the subjects they have studied. Have the students note differences between the way Taro does things (for example, going to school by public bus, carrying books in a backpack, bringing a lunch to school, having boys and girls in the same gym class) and the way things are done in their native countries. Encourage the student to note similarities as well, and point out that even though there are differences, there are basic similarities: People in all cultures care about their health, their children, their families, earning a living, getting an education, having fun, being safe, and so on.

Taking a Survey. Have the students survey the different forms of transportation used to come to school, asking *How do you come to school?* Have the students make a bar graph to display the results. See the sample bar graph form on page 13.

Doing Research. Have the students find out and report the answers to questions about your school. Use the following questions and/or create your own.

1. How many students go to this school?
2. How many classes are there for each grade level?
3. How many teachers are there? Secretaries? Custodians?
4. Who is the principal of this school?
5. How old is this school?
6. Where did the school name come from?
7. What are the school colors?
8. Is there a school motto? What is it?
9. Is there a school song? Learn it.

Creative Expression.

1. Have the students imagine that Taro wrote a story about his first day at school. Elicit first-person sentences from the class. Help the students with past-tense verb forms, such as *come/came; go/went; feel/felt; do/did; speak/spoke; understand/understood; make/made;* and *help/helped.* Read the story together when it is finished. Stage 1 students can copy the story from the blackboard. More-advanced students can elaborate on it and add more detail.

2. Have the students discuss how their first day in an American school was similar to or different from Taro's. Then have them write about their own first day. (In EFL classrooms, let the students imagine their first day of school in the United States—or teach the future tense and have them write about what they plan to do on their first day when they visit the United States.)

3. Have the students write a description of the school.

CHAPTER 4: THE FIRST AFTERNOON

Question Bank

Ask Stage 1 and Stage 2 questions as needed, in addition to the following questions.

  ++ How did Taro get home? (by bus, with his father)

  + Can Mr. Yamada take Taro to school tomorrow? (no)

+++ Why not? (because he must go to work)

  + Can Mrs. Yamada take Taro to school tomorrow? (no)

+++ Why not? (She must go with Yoko.)

  ++ Where will she go with Yoko? (to Yoko's school)

+++ Why did Taro feel sick? (He didn't want to go to school alone.)

+++ What made Taro feel better? (He said *gambaro.* It is not easy, but I can do it.)

+++ What is on Taro's I.D. card? (his name, address, and telephone number)

++++ Why is an I.D. card important?

  ++ What is your address?

  ++ What is your telephone number?

++++ Why is it dangerous to talk to strangers?

Predictive Questions for Chapter 5:

+++ What will Taro do the next morning?

  ++ Will it be a sunny day or a rainy day?

+++ What will Taro take to school with him?

+++ Where will he get on the bus?

Activity Sheets

4a. Listen and Circle (Stages 1–4)

• Have the students circle the letter of the picture that shows what you are saying.

1. *At last it was three o'clock.* (d)
2. *"I will show you how to come home by bus," said Mr. Yamada.* (a)
3. *"Get off the bus when you see a big white gas station."* (b)
4. *"It's OK," said Taro. "I can go to school by myself."* (b)
5. *"Be careful," Taro's father said. "Don't talk to strangers."* (c)
6. *This is Taro's address.* (a)

  See additional suggestions provided for Activity Sheet 1a on pages 15–16.

4b. What Are They Saying? (Stages 1–4)

• Say these sentences in random order. Have the students point to the correct picture.

1. *I must go to **work** tomorrow.* (picture 1)
2. ***I must go with** Yoko.* (picture 2)
3. *It **is not easy**, but **I can do it**.* (picture 3)
4. *This **is your** I.D. card. **Keep it in your pocket.*** (picture 4)

• Have the students look at the pictures and tell what the people are saying.

- Say the above sentences in order. Have the students write the missing words in the blanks.

- Have the students write in their own words what the people are saying.

4c. Complete the I.D. Cards (Stages 1–4)

- Help the students fill in the I.D. cards for themselves with their correct addresses and telephone numbers. Have them cut out the cards and write other useful information on the back (parents' work phone numbers, a neighbor's phone number, etc.). Laminate the cards or cover them with clear Con-Tact® paper. Tell the students to keep their I.D. cards with them at all times.
- Teach the terms *first name* and *last name*. Have the students fill in the I.D. card for Ramón Soto, using the information given in the pictures.

Answers:

IDENTIFICATION		
Ramón	Soto	
First name	Last name	
4275 Woodside Ave.		
Address		
New York	N.Y.	11379
City	State	Zip code
(718) 555-9876		
Telephone		

Extension Activities

Identification: Stating Your Name, Age, Address, and Telephone Number. Demonstrate that the terms *last name* and *first name* may have different meanings in different cultures. Taro's first name in Japanese is Yamada, which is his family name. Explain that in English the first name is our own personal name (the name that friends call us). The last name is the family name (the name that everyone in the family has).

Have the students practice asking and answering questions about their first and last names, ages, addresses, and telephone numbers.

Discovering Grammar. Point out that when you tell someone to do something, you use the basic form of the verb for a command—and *don't* plus the basic form for a negative command. Make a chart with affirmative and negative commands from the novel and from TPR activities you have done in class.

Time. Talk about the use of clocks and time in the story of Taro. Ask questions such as *What time did Taro get out of school?* and *What time do you get out of school?* Give the students small card clocks with movable hands, or have them make clocks from paper plates with paper fasteners, and movable oaktag hands. Call out times and have the students set their clocks, raising the clock faces toward you for instant feedback.

Have the students write down their important daily activities and draw a clock to show the usual time for each activity. Have them write sentences such as *I wake up at 7 o'clock; I go to school at 8 o'clock;* and *I eat lunch at 12 o'clock.*

Safety. Clarify the meaning of the word *stranger.* Explain that young people should not talk to strangers in public places. They should never go with a stranger or give a stranger information about their address or their family. Explain that people who offer children candy, money, or other treats or who invite a child to go somewhere with them can be dangerous. Children should not believe a person who says their parent sent him or her to pick them up—even a person they know. Tell the students to run away from strangers who try to talk to them and tell their parent, teacher, or principal immediately.

Sharing Culture. Ask the students questions such as *What time does school start in your country? What time is school over? How much homework do the students have? How many students are usually in a class? What did you like about school in your native country? What didn't you like? What do you like about this school? What don't you like?* If you have students from several different countries, have the students ask each other questions about school life in other countries. In EFL classrooms, give the students information about schools in the United States. Generally, the U.S. school day starts at nine and ends at three, but different places and levels may have different times.

Doing Research. Have the students study a map that shows the school neighborhood. Then walk around the neighborhood, noticing the locations (and learning the English names) of landmarks such as schools, gas stations, stores, post office, traffic lights, bus stops, parking lots, and so on. In class, have the students create a poster-size map of the neighborhood, indicating the landmarks with symbols and a key.

Self-Expression. Have the students draw pictures showing one of their surprises or first impressions about their new school. Have them talk about their pictures in pairs. Then have them write about the experience. (EFL students can draw a picture of something they like very much (or would like to change) about your school, talk about it with a partner, and then write about it.

CHAPTER 5: THE SECOND MORNING

Question Bank

Ask Stage 1 and Stage 2 questions as needed, in addition to the following questions.

++ What did Taro eat for breakfast? (rice and soup)

+++ What did the weatherman say? (It will rain very hard today.)

++ What language did the weatherman speak? (Japanese)

++ What was the weather that morning? (It was sunny.)

+++ What did Taro think? (The weatherman made a mistake.)

+++ What did Taro's mother say at eight o'clock? (It's time to go to school.)

+++ What three questions did Taro's mother ask him? (Do you have your lunch? Do you have your books? Do you have money for the bus?)

+++ What question did Taro's mother *not* ask him? (Do you have your I.D. card?)

++++ Why didn't she ask him? (Because the telephone rang, and she answered it. Taro didn't wait.)

++ Where was Taro's I.D. card? (I don't know.)

+++ What did Taro do next? (He said good-bye and walked to the corner.)

Pre_____ Questions for Chapter 6:

+ ___ ou think Taro took the wrong bus?

+++ What will Taro do at school in the morning?

+++ What will happen at lunchtime?

++ Will Taro see any of the other students?

Activity Sheets

5a. Listen and Circle (Stages 1–4)

• Have the students circle the letter of the picture that shows what you are saying.

1. *The next morning Taro got up early.* (b)

2. *He got dressed.* (b)

3. *It was a sunny day. There were no clouds.* (b)

4. *"Do you have your lunch?" asked Taro's mother.* (a)

5. *"Yes, I have money for the bus," said Taro.* (d)

6. *A bus came and Taro got on it.* (d)

See additional suggestions provided for Activity Sheet 1a on pages 15–16.

5b. What Do You See? (Stages 1–4)

• Have the students look at the picture and say the names of the things they see.

• Have the students read the words, find each object in the picture, and write the correct letter next to each word.

Answers:

1. E, 2. F, 3. H, 4. D, 5. A, 6. B, 7. C, 8. G

• In pairs or small groups, have the students tell about the actions in the picture.

- Discuss cultural differences in table manners. (For example: In Japan, people drink soup. In many other countries, people eat soup with a spoon.)
- Use the picture to teach additional vocabulary such as prepositions *(in, on, under, next to)* and the names of foods and furniture.

5c. Tell about Your Morning (Stages 1–3)

- Have the students cut the page into sentence strips and arrange the strips to show the order in which they do these activities in the morning. (The order will vary from student to student.)

- Have the students cut on the solid vertical lines to separate the sentences from the pictures. Let them play concentration in pairs, matching the sentences with the correct pictures.

- Point out that when we talk about things that we do repeatedly, or every day, we use present-tense verbs, but when we talk about something we did in the past, we use past-tense verbs. Have the students copy the sentences and then write them in the past tense.
- Have the students write paragraphs, using the sentences on the activity sheet and adding their own details and additional sentences. For example: *I get up at seven o'clock. I eat toast and cheese for breakfast.*

- Have the students draw comic strips to show the order of the things they do each morning before school. Have them talk with a partner about their pictures. Have each student write a paragraph about his or her morning and then read it to the class.

Extension Activities

Visualization and TPR: Morning Activities. Say and model the following: *You are sleeping. Wake up. Open your eyes. Yawn. Stretch. Sit up. Get out of bed. Walk to the bathroom. Wash your face. Brush your teeth. Comb your hair. Walk back to your bedroom. Make your bed. Take off your pajamas. Put on your underwear. Put on your shirt. Put on your jeans. Put on your socks. Put on your shoes.*

Walk to the kitchen. Open a cabinet. Take out some cereal. Open the box. Pour it into a bowl. Go to the refrigerator. Open the refrigerator door. Get some milk. Close the door. Open a drawer. Get a spoon. Close the drawer. Go to the table. Sit down. Pour the milk on the cereal. Eat the cereal.

Stand up. Put your dishes in the sink. Find your books. Put your books in your book bag. Put your book bag on your back. Take your lunch. Take money for the bus. Put it in your right pocket. Take your I.D. card. Put it in your left pocket. Go to the door. Say good-bye.

Discovering Grammar. Point out the word order and the use of *do* in questions. Make a chart of affirmative statements and corresponding question forms in the present and past tenses. Example: *I have my lunch. Do you have your lunch?*

Sharing Culture: Breakfast. Ask what the students eat for breakfast. Have ESL students tell if they eat the same thing in the U.S. that they ate in their native countries. Are there some breakfast foods that people don't usually eat at other times of the day? (In the U.S., cold or hot cereal, pancakes, French toast, fried eggs, toast, bacon, and sausage are typical breakfast foods. Orange juice is a popular breakfast drink. Many children drink milk and adults drink coffee with breakfast.)

Taking a Survey. Have the students take surveys of people's favorite breakfast foods/drinks and make bar graphs to show the results.

School Needs. Ask: *What did Taro need for school? What do you need to bring to school?* Review or teach the names of various class texts and supplies such as pens, pencils, paper, notebooks, erasers, scissors, crayons, glue, markers, and rulers.

Doing Research: Weather.

1. Each day of class, call attention to the weather outside. Have the students observe the clouds, wind, rain, and so on. Write a weather statement on the board each day. Have the students keep a weather calendar. Teach the two common expressions for asking about the weather: *How's the weather?* and *What's the weather like?*

2. Have more-advanced students observe different kinds of clouds and name them: cirrus, cumulus, stratus, nimbus. Have the students check a thermometer outside the window and/or a wind sock, barometer, or rain gauge. Record the temperature each day. Have one group of students draw a line graph of the temperatures for a month, and another group draw a bar graph showing the number of days that are sunny, partly sunny, cloudy, rainy, and so on.

3. Ask ESL students about the typical weather this month in their native countries.

Sharing Culture: Weather. Teach the poems small children chant on rainy days: "Rain, rain, go away! Come again another day" and "It's raining, it's pouring; The old man is snoring. He bumped his head when he went to bed, and he didn't get up in the morning." Have the students share any equivalent rhymes about rain from their native languages.

Money. Teach the names and values of U.S. coins, using either real coins or play money. Have the students figure the value of various combinations of coins. Then have them figure what coin combinations could work for a thirty-cent telephone call, a fifty-cent bag of peanuts, a bus ride at a dollar and a quarter, a school lunch, and so on.

CHAPTER 6: TARO MAKES FRIENDS

Question Bank

Ask Stage 1 and Stage 2 questions as needed, in addition to the following questions.

+++ What problem did Taro have with the teachers? (They spoke too fast.)

++ What did Taro say to himself to feel better? (*Gambaro.* It is not easy, but I can do it.)

+++ What were three things Taro did in the morning? (He copied words from the blackboard. He looked at the pictures in his books. He tried to listen to the teachers.)

++ Who did Taro sit next to at lunchtime? (Ramón and Lee)

++++ Why did Taro bring eight rice balls for lunch? (to share with the other students)

++++ What did the other students give Taro? (Ramón gave him a taco, Lee gave him an egg roll, Susan gave him half her sandwich, Jae Han gave him an apple.)

+++ What did Susan say to some other students? (Come meet Taro.)

+++ Who else did Taro meet? (Jean-Claude Bienami, Milo Wyborna, Carmen Lopez, and Bao Tran)

+++ Where were the other students from? (Jean-Claude was from Haiti, Milo was from Poland, Carmen was from Puerto Rico, and Bao was from Vietnam.)

+++ Why was Taro happy? (He had new friends.)

Predictive Questions for Chapter 7:

++ What subjects do you think Taro will study in the afternoon?

+ Do you think the afternoon will be difficult for Taro?

+++ What do you think the weather will be like after school?

++++ What do you think will happen to Taro?

Activity Sheets

6a. Listen and Circle (Stages 1–4)

• Have the students circle the letter of the picture that shows what you are saying.

1. *In fifteen minutes, the bus arrived at Taro's school.* (b)

2. *Taro copied words from the blackboard.* (b)

3. *Taro gave one rice ball to each boy and girl.* (d)

4. *Susan gave Taro half her sandwich.* (d)

5. *"Come meet Taro," Susan said to some other students.* (c)

6. *"Taro, this is Bao Tran. She doesn't speak English either," said Susan.* (a)

See additional suggestions provided for Activity Sheet 1a on pages 15–16.

6b. Choose the Best Sentence (Stages 1, 2)

- Have the students look at each picture and circle the letter of the sentence that best tells about the picture.

Answers:

1. a, 2. b, 3. b, 4. a.

6c. Complete the Sentences (Stages 1–4)

- Have the students read the paragraph and fill in the blanks with words from the word bank.

Answers:

1. teachers, 2. talked, 3. I, 4. words, 5. pictures, 6. listen, 7. lunchtime

Extension Activities

Visualization and TPR: Going to School. Say and model the following: *Go out the door. Walk to the corner. Wait for a bus. Get on the bus. Sit on a seat. Look out the window. Get up. Walk to the front of the bus. Get off the bus. Go into the school. Sit down at your desk. Open your book. Listen to the teacher. Copy words from the blackboard.*

Discovering Grammar. Point out *he's, she's, doesn't,* and other contractions used in the novel. Explain the use of the apostrophe (') to show where letters have been omitted.

Food. Use picture cards to teach the names of foods such as fruits and vegetables, salad, soup, spaghetti, rice, bread, sandwich, milk, and juice. Have the students tell what they eat for lunch. Ask what new foods they have learned to eat in the United States (or what foods they would like to eat if they went to the United States). Discuss "junk food" (sugary or fat-filled food) and its consequences: low energy, tooth cavities, poor nutrition, weight gain, pimples). Plan a "picnic" lunch or snack in the classroom, with each student bringing a healthful item such as raw carrots, salad, fruit, raisins, crackers, and juice. Be sure to provide napkins, paper cups, and plates.

Introductions. Have groups of students role-play the scene in which Susan introduces several students to Taro. Then have them practice introducing a partner to the rest of the class.

Sharing Culture: Meals. Have the students discuss common foods, school lunchroom facilities, and eating customs in their native countries. Ask questions such as *Do people eat with forks, spoons, and knives? Do people sit at tables? Do families eat together, or do some people eat separately? What time do people eat each meal? How many meals a day do people eat? Are there foods that people will not eat? Who cooks in most families? Who shops for food? Do students eat at school or go home to eat? Do they eat with their teachers, in their classrooms? Are free lunches available at schools?* Explain that Americans come from different backgrounds and have many different customs. Both mothers and fathers may shop for food and cook in some families; most students eat lunch at school, in large lunchrooms. Their teachers usually do not eat lunch with them. Some people in the United States are vegetarians and do not eat meat; many American Jewish people do not eat pork or shellfish; Muslims do not eat beef. Some people do not eat junk food.

Doing Research: Countries of Origin.

1. Using a world map, locate the native countries of your students and perhaps their parents. Mark them with stars or thumbtacks. Have the students create a bar graph of their origins. Review or teach the names of your students' native countries, nationalities, and native languages, plus those of Taro and his new friends.

2. Have the students find out your school's ethnic population statistics, and make a bar graph to display their data. If this information isn't readily available, have the students do direct research by creating a small census form, duplicating it (six or

eight copies to a sheet of paper), and distributing it to every class in the school. (If the school is very large, take a census of a particular grade instead.) Have the students make a bar graph and share the information they have gathered.

3. In EFL classes, teach the English names of countries in the news and have the students find the countries on a world map. Teach them the English words for each country's nationality and the language(s) spoken there.

Self-Expression: Food. Have the students draw pictures of their favorite foods and talk about their pictures with a partner. Have each one write a paragraph about the foods he or she likes.

CHAPTER 7: TARO GOES HOME BY HIMSELF

Question Bank

Ask Stage 1 and Stage 2 questions as needed, in addition to the following questions.

++ What classes did Taro have in the afternoon? (math and gym)

+++ What subjects do you need the most English for? (social studies, science, literature)

+++ What subjects do you need the least? (gym, art, math)

+++ How was the weather outside after school? (cloudy and windy)

+++ What is our weather like today?

++++ What did Taro think now about the weatherman? (He was right.)

+++ What did Taro and Ramón do while they were waiting for the bus? (They played catch with a ball.)

++ Did Taro check the number of the bus? (no)

++ Who sat next to him on the bus? (Ramón)

++ What did Ramón say when he got off the bus? (Bye, Taro. See you tomorrow.)

++ What did Taro look for? (a big white gas station)

Predictive Questions for Chapter 8:

+++ What do you think will happen next?

+++ What will Taro do?

+++ What will the bus driver do?

+ Will it rain?

Activity Sheets

7a. Listen and Circle (Stages 1–4)

- Have the students circle the letter of the picture that shows what you are saying.

1. *Taro was good in math.* (a)
2. *It was cloudy now. It was very windy.* (b)
3. *Taro caught the ball.* (d)
4. *Everyone got on the bus.* (a)
5. *Taro sat next to a window. Ramón sat next to him.* (d)
6. *Taro's friends got off the bus.* (d)

See additional suggestions provided for Activity Sheet 1a on pages 15–16.

7b. What Are They Doing? (Stages 1–3)

- Have the students tell about each picture, using the present continuous tense. Point out that when we read or tell a story, we usually use the past tense, but when we describe a picture or tell what is happening now, we use present continuous verb forms. Contrast the two tenses in two columns on the blackboard.

- Have the students write a sentence that tells what is happening in each picture, using words from the word bank.

Answers:
1. He is throwing the ball.
2. He is catching the ball.
3. They are waiting for the bus.
4. They are getting on the bus.
5. She is sitting on the bus.
6. They are getting off the bus.

7c. What Happened First? (Stages 1–3)

- Have the students cut the page into sentence strips and arrange the strips in order to tell the story.

  Answers:

  1. At last, it was three o'clock. The boys and girls went outside.
  2. Taro walked to the bus stop with his friends.
  3. Soon a bus came. Everyone got on the bus.
  4. Taro got on the bus, too. He sat next to the window.
  5. Ramón sat next to him.
  6. Ramón got up. He said, "Bye, Taro. See you tomorrow."

- Have the students cut on the solid vertical lines to separate the pictures from the sentences. Have them mix up the pictures and then match them with the correct sentences. They might play concentration with a partner, matching the sentences with the correct pictures.

- Have the students look only at the pictures and tell the story in their own words.

- Have the students write a sentence for each picture.

Extension Activities

Total Physical Response: Baseball and Other Sports. Say and model the following: *You are going to play a game. It's baseball. Take a bat. Get ready to swing. Here comes the ball. Swing. You missed. Swing again. You hit it! Run to first base. Run to second base. Run to third base. Run home. It's a home run!* Use a similar procedure for other sports.

Make paper balls by crushing paper together and wrapping a strip of masking tape around it. Have the students play catch in groups of five or six, using the phrases, *Catch!, Throw it to me, Got it, Missed it, Too high,* and *Too low.*

School Subjects. Elicit the names of school subjects from the students; write them on the board and have the students learn the correct spelling for each one. Have the students write out their schedules and tell which are their favorite subjects.

Weather. Continue the class weather calendar. Add weather words as they occur: fog, wind, storm, hurricane, blizzard, lightning, thunder.

Taking a Survey. Ask the students what their favorite sports are. Have them make bar graphs to show the favorite sports in the class. Have several students explain their bar graphs.

Sharing Culture. Have the students talk about public transportation in various countries. What are good manners on a bus in the United States? (Sit quietly. Move to the back of the bus when standing. If your bus is full, give your seat to an elderly or disabled person or a person with a baby. Don't disturb the driver or talk to him while he is driving.) What are good manners on a bus in other countries?

Self-Expression: Friends. Have the students draw pictures of their first friend (or their first friend in the United States). Have them talk about their pictures in pairs and tell how they became friends with this person. Have each student write a paragraph about his or her first friend.

CHAPTER 8: TARO IS LOST

Question Bank

Ask Stage 1 and Stage 2 questions as needed, in addition to the following questions.

- \+ Was Taro on the wrong bus? (yes)
- \++ What did the bus driver do? (He stopped the bus.)
- \++ How was the weather now? (It was dark and very windy.)
- \++ Who did Taro want to call? (his mother)
- \++ Did Taro have his I.D. card in his pocket? (no)

+++ Where was it? (I don't know. He left it at home.)

++ Did Taro know his address or his telephone number? (no)

+++ Do you know Taro's address or telephone number?

++ Do you know your address and your telephone number?

++++ What are four problems Taro has? (He's lost. He doesn't know his phone number or his address. He doesn't speak English. It's going to rain very hard.)

Predictive Questions for Chapter 9:

++ Will Taro ask someone for help?

++++ Since Taro doesn't speak English, how can he ask?

++ Who will help him?

+ Will it rain?

++++ What will Taro do if it rains?

Activity Sheets

8a. Listen and Circle (Stages 1–4)

- Have the students circle the letter of the picture that shows what you are saying.
  1. *This person is a bus driver.* (b)
  2. *Taro got up. He spoke to the bus driver.* (a)
  3. *The wind blew papers and cans in the street.* (b)
  4. *Taro put his hand in his pocket to get his I.D. card.* (d)
  5. *Oh, no! The I.D. card was not in his pocket.* (b)
  6. *Taro didn't know his address.* (a)

  See additional suggestions provided for Activity Sheet 1a on pages 15–16.

8b. What Do You See? (Stages 1–4)

- Elicit from the students the names of all the objects they see in the picture. Have them tell what the people in the picture are doing.

- Have the students read the words, find each object in the picture, and write the correct letter next to each word.

Answers:

1. E, 2. I, 3. B, 4. C, 5. H, 6. G, 7. A, 8. D, 9. F

- Discuss traffic safety and rules on the street such as crossing with a crossing guard or at a corner, obeying traffic lights and signs, not jaywalking (crossing in the middle of the street), using litter baskets, cleaning up after one's dog, and so forth. Ask what rules there are on the street in other countries.

- Use the picture to teach additional vocabulary, such as word order (subject, verb, object, or prepositional phrase: *A woman is carrying an umbrella; A crossing guard is stopping a car; A girl is getting on the bus* and transportation words *(car, bicycle, bus, walking)*.

- Have the students write five sentences about the picture.

- Have the students draw a picture of a street they know well (for example, the street they live on, the street the school is on, or a street in their native country). Have the students talk about their pictures with a partner. Have the students write paragraphs about their streets and share their paragraphs with several partners. Post the paragraphs for the class to read.

Extension Activities

Total Physical Response: Finding Things. Say and model the following: *Where did you put your I.D. card? Look in your desk. Take out your notebook. Look in your notebook. Take out your pencil case. Look in your pencil case. Take out your other books. Look in your other books. Look* *in your pocket. Oh no! Your I.D. card isn't in your pocket. Look in the other pocket. It's not there, either. Look in all of your pockets. You can't find your I.D. card. Pull your hair.*

Discovering Grammar. Point out the subject pronouns in the novel and their possessive adjective forms and objective forms. Make a chart showing these forms: *I, my, me; he, his, him.*

Coping Skills. Elicit from the students how Taro coped in school with no English. (He tried to listen; he copied words from the blackboard; he looked at pictures.) How did he cope with making friends? (He sat with them at lunchtime; he brought food to share.) Have the students make a list of things that would help a person who is lost. (Examples: one's address and telephone number; the name and telephone number of a neighbor; the telephone number of a parent at work; the telephone number for the police station; the ability to use a telephone; the ability to ask for directions; money for a bus; the ability to read a map; knowledge of city geography; an umbrella; a jacket; knowing not to talk to strangers.)

Problem-Solving Skills: Brainstorming. Teach the students how to brainstorm solutions to problems. (In a brainstorming session, each suggestion is written down but not judged. At first, the number of ideas is more important than the quality of the ideas. A good idea may be right behind a silly one, so you have to say the silly idea to get at the better one.) Set a time limit, such as six minutes, and a minimum number of solutions, such as twenty. Keep going past the time limit, if the students are still coming up with fruitful responses. When a large number of ideas has been generated, have the students evaluate each idea.

Sample brainstorming session: What are some ways Taro could get home?

- Try to take a taxi—draw pictures to show a taxi driver, his mother crying, his house near the big white gas station, and his father with money.
- Go to a store and ask the storekeeper for help.
- Ask a person on the street to call the police for him.

Practice brainstorming other problems, including problems or issues in your own school. Examples: How can the school make sure that newcomers don't get lost on their first day of school? What are ways to help newcomers stop worrying? How can this classroom be improved?

CHAPTER 9: THE STORM BEGINS

Question Bank

Ask Stage 1 and Stage 2 questions as needed, in addition to the following questions.

+++ Why were people walking quickly? (They didn't want to get wet in the rain.)

++ What did Taro ask the woman with the small boy? (Ja-ku-son Hai-tsu?)

++ Could she understand him? (no)

+++ What was the weather like now? (The clouds got darker. The wind blew harder.)

++ What did Taro say to himself? (*Gambaro.* It is not easy, but I can do it.)

++++ How did Taro get to the bus stop? (Two girls took him there.)

++++ What happened then? (Taro waited, but the number three bus didn't come. It began to rain.)

++ Where did Taro go? (under some stairs)

+++ How bad was the storm? (Very bad. Cars turned on their lights. Then cars could not go.)

+++ What happened under the stairs? (The rain made a lake under the stairs.)

Predictive Questions for Chapter 10:

++ Who do you think can help Taro?

++ Do you think Taro's mother is worried?

+++ What do you think she will do?

++ Who do you think she will call?

Activity Sheets

9a. Listen and Circle (Stages 1–4)

- Have the students circle the letter of the picture that shows what you are saying.

  1. *Many people were on the street. They were walking quickly.* (d)

2. *Taro saw a woman with a small boy.*
(b)

3. *The number seven bus came.* (d)

4. *It began to rain.* (a)

5. *Everyone in the street was running.* (c)

6. *Taro's shoes were wet. His socks were wet. And his feet were very, very wet.* (b)

See additional suggestions provided for Activity Sheet 1a on pages 15–16.

9b. Make New Conversations (Stages 2, 3)

- Have the students read the conversation in pairs. Point out the underlined words. Demonstrate that the students are to make new conversations by substituting words from the word bank in place of the underlined words. Have one partner ask the questions while the other answers, then switch.

9c. Ask for and Give Directions (Stages 3, 4)

- Have the students work in pairs, using two maps. Have them read and follow the directions. Demonstrate how to glue the pictures on the squares with the same letters (A or B).

Extension Activities

Total Physical Response: Adverbs. Say and model the following: *Walk. Walk quickly. Walk slowly. Run. Run slowly. Run quickly. Jump. Jump slowly. Jump quickly. Swim. Swim quickly. Swim slowly. Talk quickly. (What's your name?) Talk slowly. (W h a t ' s . . . y o u r . . . n a m e?) Talk softly. Talk loud.*

Total Physical Response: Parts of the Body. Say and model the following: *Touch your head. Touch your eyes. Touch your nose. Touch your mouth. Clap your hands. Clap your elbows. Pull your hair. Pull your ears. Wiggle your fingers. Wiggle your toes. Wiggle your nose.* Have the students draw a body and label the parts.

Discovering Grammar. Continue your personal pronoun chart. Add *she, her, her; they, their, them.*

Numbers Review.

1. Have the students count by tens, fives, twos, threes, and so forth.

2. With students in fourth grade and up, play the game of Buzz. The students sit in a circle (you can have two games going if your class is large). One student begins to count, and each person says the next number, except that a student must say *buzz* instead of any number with seven in it or any multiple of seven. (Example: one, two, three, four, five, six, *buzz*, eight, nine, ten, eleven, twelve, thirteen, *buzz*, fifteen, sixteen, *buzz*, eighteen, nineteen, twenty, *buzz*, etc.)

3. Write a row of three-digit numbers on the blackboard and have the students practice reading them. Then send several students to the blackboard and dictate three-digit numbers for them to write as the other students write them at their seats.

4. Point out the different ways of reading numbers in street addresses and telephone numbers. Example: Seven hundred eighteen (718) may be said as "seven eighteen" in an address and "seven one eight" in a phone number.

Asking for and Giving Directions. Have the students practice asking for and giving directions from the school to some familiar local landmarks.

CHAPTER 10: TARO'S FAMILY WORRIES

Question Bank

Ask Stage 1 and Stage 2 questions as needed, in addition to the following questions.

+++ What did Mrs. Yamada and Yoko do at three-thirty? (They went to the big white gas station.

+++ What happened at four-thirty? (It began to rain.)

++++ Why was Taro's mother worried? (Taro did not come home.)

++ Who did Mrs. Yamada speak to at the school? (the principal)

++ What did Mrs. Yamada ask? (Where is Yamada Taro?)

++ What did the principal say? (Taro went home at three o'clock.)

++++ What did the principal say he would do? (He said he would make some phone calls.)

++ Who did Mrs. Yamada call then? (Mr. Yamada)

++ What did she tell him? (Taro didn't come home from school.)

++ What did Mr. Yamada say? (I'll be right there.)

Predictive Questions for Chapter 11:

+ Will the Yamadas call the police?

+++ How will they find out where Taro is?

+++ How will they describe Taro?

+++ What was Taro wearing?

Activity Sheets

10a. What Are They Saying? (Stages 1–4)

- Have the students listen as you read the quotations below. Have them point to or raise their hands to tell you the number of the picture that goes with each quotation.
  1. *"Did Taro take his I.D. card with him?"* (picture 4)
  2. *"It's four-thirty. Where is Taro?"* (picture 1)
  3. *"Taro went home at three o'clock."* (picture 3)
  4. *"Taro didn't come home from school."* (picture 2)

- Dictate the sentences above and have the students write each sentence in the correct word balloon.

- Have the students think about what the people are saying and write it in the word balloons in their own words.

10b. Unscramble the Words (Stages 2, 3)

- Teach the concept of unscrambling letters to find a word. Then have the students read the paragraph, unscrambling the missing words and writing them on the lines.

  Answers:
  1. three-thirty, 2. gas station, 3. waited, 4. Many, 5. began, 6. worried, 7. house

Extension Activities

Discovering Grammar. Give examples of verbs that are followed by other verbs and the particle *to*: It *began to rain.* Taro *didn't want to go* to school by himself. He *tried to listen.* Have students give other examples from the novel or create new sentences.

Telephone Calls. Teach or review the following telephone procedures, as appropriate to your students' ages and language abilities.

- how to distinguish the dial tone, the ringing sound, and the busy signal
- how to call the police and fire departments and ambulance
- how to report emergencies, fires, accidents, or crimes
- how to call Information to request a phone number
- how to call Information in a different city
- when to use area codes and when they are not necessary
- how to leave a message on an answering machine, including their name, the time they called, and their telephone number
- how to use a pay telephone
- how to call collect
- how to distinguish common recorded messages, and understand typical operator language
- how to call to make an appointment with a doctor or dentist

Time. Extend the students' ability to tell time by introducing the concept of the half hour. Have the students work with their clocks to show three-thirty, four-thirty, and so on.

Sharing Culture. Have the students tell what they say in their own language when they answer the telephone. What are good telephone manners in their native countries?

Doing Research. Teach the students how to read a bus schedule and a bus route map. Plan a class trip by bus. Have the students follow the route on a city map.

CHAPTER 11: THE PRINCIPAL CALLS FOR HELP

Question Bank

Ask Stage 1 and Stage 2 questions as needed, in addition to the following questions.

++ Where did Taro's mother and father go? (to Taro's school)

++ Who did the principal call? (the students in Taro's class)

+++ What did Ramón tell the principal? (Taro was on our bus. We didn't know he was on the wrong bus.)

+++ What did the principal ask Ramón to do? (Tell your parents. Come to the school.)

++++ Then what happened? (Ramón called Lee. Lee called Susan. Susan called Jean-Claude; and so forth.)

++ Who did the principal call? (the police)

++++ What does Taro look like? (He is four feet, eleven inches tall; he has short, straight black hair and black eyes.)

+++ What was Taro wearing? (He was wearing a white shirt, a blue sweater, and jeans.)

++ What did Taro's father give to the police officers? (a picture of Taro)

++++ Why did the principal call the TV stations? (He was very worried. He wanted the TV stations to tell people to help find Taro.)

Predictive Questions for Chapter 12:

+ Do you think the rain is going to stop?

+ Do you think Taro's bus (number three) is going to come?

+++ How will Taro know when to get off the bus?

++ Will Taro get something to eat?

Activity Sheets

11a. Read and Color (Stages 1–3)

• Have the students read the text. Have them draw and color to finish the picture, using the information they read.

• Cover the text before photocopying and use this sheet as a listening activity. To increase the challenge add other details, such as *Draw three buttons on Milo's shirt, Draw a large pocket on Milo's pants,* and *Draw a brown dog next to Milo.*

• Have the students write a description of Milo after they have finished the picture.

11b. Play a Guessing Game (Stages 1–4)

• Have the students read the rules of the game. Play the game as a class until most of the students understand how to play and how to ask appropriate questions. Then divide the class into groups of three to five students to continue playing. Circulate to check sentence structure and assist as needed. To increase the difficulty level, have the students answer in complete sentences: *No, she doesn't have blonde hair; Yes, she is wearing glasses; No, it isn't Anna;* and so forth.

• Have the students choose three faces and write a description of each one. Tell them to write the names that go with the faces on a separate sheet of paper. Have them exchange papers with a partner, read each other's descriptions, and guess the names of the people their partner has written about.

11c. Describe Yourself (Stages 1–4)

- Have the students work in pairs and take turns interviewing each other. After answering their partner's questions orally, have them work individually to complete the paragraph about themselves. To increase the difficulty level, have the students add details of character, personality, hobbies, likes, and dislikes to their personal descriptions. Have them draw pictures of themselves as well.

  Tell the students not to write their names on their papers. Post the papers, giving each a number. Have the students each make a list of the numbers and write the name of the person they think is described in each paper. Next write the numbers on the blackboard and ask the class, *Who do you think number 1 is?* Then ask the student (or students) named to confirm the other students' guesses.

Extension Activities

Offering to Help. Teach the students to say and respond to phrases such as *May I help you? How can I help? Can I help?* and *Do you need any help?* (*Yes, thank you. You're very kind.* or *No, thank you. I can manage.*)

Discovering Grammar. Point out that the verb *can* is followed by a verb, but there is no particle *to* after *can*. Demonstrate that the past form of *can* is *could*. Elicit sentences with *can* and write them on the board.

Describing a Person. Bring a scale, small hand mirrors, and a tape measure or yardstick to class. Teach the English measuring system (*inches, feet, miles, pounds,* and *ounces*). Mark off feet and inches on a wall or door and have the students measure each other. Let the students weigh themselves. Then have them describe themselves in English: I am ___ feet ___ inches tall. I weigh ____ pounds. Have the students take turns describing a "mystery person" from the class, telling height, weight, hair and eye color, and color of clothes. The rest of the class should guess who the speaker is talking about. Be sensitive and supportive of students who might feel too tall, short, small, or heavy. Avoid the use of labels such as *fat* or *skinny*.

Colors. Review or teach the color names in English. Include *navy blue, tan, gray, pink,* and so on, as needed.

Clothing. Review or teach the names of articles of clothing. Have the students describe what they and others are wearing. Add color words and other vocabulary (*plaid, striped, flowered, plain, short-sleeved, long-sleeved,* etc.) as appropriate.

Paper People. Bring in a roll of large poster paper. Have the students work in pairs, one lying on the paper with arms spread slightly, and the other tracing the shape of the body on the paper. Then have the partners switch places. Do the tracing yourself for younger students who can't trace accurately. Have the students cut out their life-size replicas, draw their faces, and color their hair and clothes appropriately. Display the paper people in the classroom or hall.

  Do a TPR activity with the paper people. Examples: *Go to the boy who is wearing a blue shirt and green pants. Go to the girl who has long hair and is wearing glasses.*

  Have the students talk about their paper people in pairs, introduce them to each other, and describe them to each other.

Sharing Culture. Talk about the role of the police in your town. Discuss good manners with police officers. Ask what interactions students have had with the police. Discuss the students' feelings about the police in the Unites States and in their native countries.

Doing Research. Have the students find and report the answers to these questions: Where is the closest police station? What is the telephone number for the police? What jobs do the police do? How does someone become a police officer? What do police officers have to learn?

CHAPTER 12: STILL LOST

Question Bank

Ask Stage 1 and Stage 2 questions as needed, in addition to the following questions.

- + Did the rain stop? (It slowed down.)
- ++ Which bus came? (the number three bus)
- ++ How long was Taro on the bus? (a long time)

+++ Why did Taro get off the bus? (He saw a big white gas station.)

+++ How was the weather now? (It was raining hard again. It was very dark.)

+ Was it the right gas station? (no)

+++ Why didn't Taro wait for another bus? (He didn't have any money.)

++ How far did he walk? (many blocks)

+++ Does the stranger look kind or dangerous to you?

++ Do you think Taro should talk to him?

++++ Why or why not?

Predictive Questions for Chapter 13:

++ Who will come to the school?

++ What will the principal tell them?

++++ How will they help to look for Taro?

++ Will the TV stations tell about Taro?

Activity Sheets

12a. Choose the Best Sentence (Stages 1–3)

- Have the students read the sentences and look at the pictures. Have them circle the letter of the sentence that best describes each picture.

Answers:

1. b, 2. a, 3. b, 4. b, 5. a.

12b. How Are the Pictures Different? (Stages 3, 4)

- Have the students work individually to circle the eight items that are different in the two pictures. Then have them write sentences telling how the pictures are different. Write an example on the blackboard. Then have the students talk about the differences with a partner and compare their sentences.

Answers:

1. In A, there is a clock; there is no clock in B.

2. In A, the sign says "Joe's Gas." In B, it says "John's Gas."

3. Gas costs $1.38 and $1.48 in A. It costs $1.38 and $1.45 in B.

4. The gas station in A is on 27th Street. The gas station in B is on 127th Street.

5. The gas station in A is open. The gas station in B is closed.

6. There is a door on the left of the garage door in A. There is a door on the right of the garage door in B.

7. There is a men's room in A. There is a ladies' room in B.

8. There is a telephone in A. There is no telephone in B.

Extension Activities

Total Physical Response: Emotions. Teach the names of various feelings and emotions through body language, facial expressions, and situations. Act out different feelings and have the students guess how you feel. Then say and model TPR commands, such as *Be happy. Be sad. Be cold. Be tired. Be sick. Be hungry. Be angry. Be surprised. Be embarrassed. Be excited.*

Don't Talk to Strangers. Review the safety rules discussed in Chapter 4. Discuss Taro's reaction to the stranger, and brainstorm ways Taro could respond to him.

Discovering Grammar. Have the students notice that emotions and body states are expressed in English with the verb *be.* Examples: *I'm scared. He's hungry. They're cold.* Many other languages use different verbs that would translate as *have* and *exist,* to express these conditions.)

Sharing Culture: Showing Emotions. Have the students discuss and become aware of cultural differences in the use of language and facial expressions to show emotions. Many Americans may appear very emotional to Asians, but *un*emotional to South Americans; at the same time, Asians may appear *un*emotional to Americans. South Americans and Southern Europeans may appear very emotional to Americans. Discuss the different places or reasons that it is okay or not okay to cry, shout, laugh, or be angry in the students' cultures. Is it okay for adults/women/men to show emotions? Are some emotions considered "good" and others "bad"?

Help the students to understand that there is no single "right way" to express emotions. People are usually most comfortable with the way of expressing emotions that is practiced in their own family. In the past, American boys were commonly taught not to cry by saying, "Big boys don't cry." Girls were told to hide their anger, but it was okay for them to show fear or to cry. These attitudes are less common now, and both men and women are considered healthier if they can express their sad feelings, anger, and fears.

Self-Expression. Have the students draw pictures of things that make them feel happy, sad, angry, worried, excited, embarrassed, or some other emotion. Have them talk about their pictures with a partner. Then have them write paragraphs about their pictures.

CHAPTER 13: EVERYONE LOOKS FOR TARO

Question Bank

Ask Stage 1 and Stage 2 questions as needed, in addition to the following questions.

++ Who came to the school? (the students and their parents)

+++ What did the principal do? (He told the parents to look for Taro. He showed them a map. He told some parents to go east and some parents to go north.)

+++ What did Mr. Wong say to Mr. Yamada? (Come in our car.)

+++ What did Mrs. Soto say to Mrs. Yamada? (Come with us.)

++++ What did the parents do? (They went north and east. They called for Taro at every corner.)

++++ What did the TV stations do? (They showed Taro's picture on TV. They asked people to call if they saw Taro.)

++++ Then what happened? (No one found Taro.)

+++ What happened at ten-fifteen? (The parents went back to the school.)

++ How did everyone feel? (They were very worried.)

Predictive Questions for Chapter 14:

+ Will Taro talk to the stranger?

+++ What will happen next?

Activity Sheets

13a. Play a Guessing Game (Stages 1, 2)

• Divide the class into groups of three or more, or teams of at least two persons each. Have each group cut one sheet on the dotted lines to make sixteen cards, mix up the cards, and place them facedown in a stack. The first player takes the top card and looks at it, but does not show it to anyone else.

The player with the card must use gestures, body language, and actions to show the word that's on the card. He or she may not speak. The other students in the group or team must try to guess the word. Groups may keep score by recording how many seconds it takes to guess each word. The winning team or group is the one with the lowest score.

After becoming familiar with this game, the students can make up additional word cards to use.

13b. Draw and Guess (Stages 2, 3)

• Divide the class into groups or teams. Have each group cut out the cards on one sheet, mix them up, and place them facedown in a stack. The first player takes the top card and draws a picture of that word. The other teammates try to guess the word as they watch their teammate draw. No letters or numbers may be used in the drawings. A timekeeper records how many seconds it takes the group to guess each word. The winning team has the lowest total time.

13c. Unscramble and Match The Opposites (Stage 4)

- Review the concept of unscrambling letters to find a word. Show the students that the sheet contains pairs of words with opposite meanings. First have the students unscramble the words and write them on the lines. Then they can draw lines to connect the opposites.

    Answers:

    1. wet—e. dry
    2. small—f. big
    3. lost—h. found
    4. stop—b. begin
    5. tall—a. short
    6. friend—d. stranger
    7. came—c. went
    8. easy—g. difficult

Extension Activities

Discovering Grammar. Point out the differences in meaning between *look, look at,* and *look for; get, get on, get off, get dressed,* and *get up.*

Multi-ethnic Cooperation. Talk about the variety of ethnic groups represented by the people who came to help look for Taro. Ask: *Why are they all coming together? What ethnic groups are represented at this school? What are the advantages of knowing people in other ethnic groups? In what ways are all people alike? In what ways may groups be different? What are stereotypes? What is prejudice? How can prejudice hurt people? What are the advantages of living in a multicultural society?*

Family Values. Raise the following questions for discussion: *Are all families the same? How are families different? What are the purposes of a family? What values may families have in common?* Have the students interview their parents to learn the hopes, rules, and values of the family. *What does your family want for you? What does your family want for its future? What values can you contribute to your family?*

Reading a City Map. Post a large map of your city. Have the students locate the school, their streets, the major sections of your city, city boundaries, neighboring towns and cities, bodies of water, parks, and so on.

Doing Research. What foreign-language TV channels and radio stations are available in your town or city? Let the students recommend a favorite TV program in their native language. Have other students watch or listen to it to see how much they can understand.

Class Visit: the Police Station. Plan a trip to the local police station or invite a police officer to talk to your class. (The topic can vary with the age of the students: preventing burglary, not using drugs, not talking to strangers, what to do if they get lost, what to do in typical emergencies, etc.). Ask the officer to bring visual aids if possible; explain that the students have a small vocabulary base and need props or illustrations to make spoken English comprehensible. Pre-teach vocabulary you anticipate in the police officer's presentation.

CHAPTER 14: TARO THINKS HARD

Question Bank

Ask Stage 1 and Stage 2 questions as needed, in addition to the following questions.

++++ Why didn't Taro talk to the stranger? (He remembered his father's words.)

+++ Do you think Taro knows that his parents are looking for him?

+++ How will Taro call for help?

++ How much money do you need to make a telephone call?

++ Do you need any money to call the police?

+++ How do you call the police?

+++ What problems did Taro have when he looked for a telephone? (The first phone he saw was broken.)

++ What did Taro say to the operator? (Hello! Hello! *Moshi moshi!)*

++ What language did the second operator speak? (Japanese)

+++ What did Taro tell her? (I'm lost.)

Predictive Questions for Chapter 15:

++++ How will Taro tell the operator where he is?

+++ What will the operator do?

+++ What do you think will happen next?

Activity Sheets

14a. Use the Telephone (Stages 3, 4)

- Have the students look at the picture and study the names for the parts of a telephone. Then have the students read the directions for making a phone call, filling in the blanks with words from the top of the page.

  Answers:

  2. coin slot, 3. number buttons,
  5. coin return lever; coin return box

14b. Practice Conversations (Stages 2, 3, 4)

- Have two students read each conversation to the class. Teach any new vocabulary, such as *collect call*. Have students practice the conversations in pairs, taking turns being Taro and the operators.

- If appropriate, give the students a homework assignment of calling Information to ask for a friend's phone number.

- Show students how to find names and phone numbers listed in the telephone book.

Extension Activities

Discovering Grammar. Have the students notice the use of words that modify nouns and the order in which they appear. Examples: *many*

policemen, another phone, Japanese telephone, a long time. (In some languages, adjectives follow rather than precede the nouns they modify.)

Using the Telephone. Use a pay telephone at school. Have the students point to the parts of the telephone as you name them: *receiver, coin slot, coin return box, number buttons, mouthpiece, earpiece, wire, coin return lever, instructions.* Prearrange with someone that you will call, or call your home answering machine.

Do a TPR activity: *Pick up the receiver. Put it near your ear. Listen for the dial tone. Buzzzzzz. Deposit (___ cents). Press the numbers you want to call. Wait for the phone to ring. There's no answer. Hang up.*

Explain the meanings of telephone service recorded messages. Examples: *Your time is up. If you'd like to continue talking, please deposit another ___ cents. I'm sorry. The number you have dialed is not in service. I'm sorry, you cannot complete your call as dialed. Please hang up and dial again. This is not a working number. The number you have reached has been changed. The new number is ___ .* These messages vary, so do some checking first to prepare a list of the messages your students are likely to hear.

Telephone Survival Skills. Review the phone number(s) for calling the police and fire departments in your area. Discuss the answers to the following: How much does it cost to make a local phone call? How many numbers are in a local phone number? What is an area code? What does it mean if the line goes "beep beep beep"? How can you get your money back? How can you get help to make a call?

Sharing Culture. Some telephone companies have bilingual operators who help people make long-distance overseas calls. When a regular operator hears a person who cannot speak English, he or she calls in the language-assistance operators, who try to determine what language the caller is speaking. Then an operator who speaks that language is connected to the caller.

Brainstorming. Review the procedure for brainstorming. (Set a time limit and a number of ideas; write down every idea without evaluating it.) In small groups, have the students brainstorm ways to help new arrivals at your school. When there are many ideas written, have students choose ideas that they think will work best. Have them plan to share their ideas with others in the school.

CHAPTER 15: HOORAY! IT'S TARO

Question Bank

Ask Stage 1 and Stage 2 questions as needed, in addition to the following questions.

+++ How did the operator know where Taro was? (Taro read the letters on a street sign.)

+++ Where was Taro? (at Grand Street and Seventy-third Street)

++ What did the operator tell Taro to do? (Wait there.)

++ How soon did the police come? (in two minutes)

+++ What did the police officer do? (She put a blanket around Taro.)

++ What did Taro's friends do when they saw Taro? (They cheered.)

++ What did Taro's parents do? (They hugged him.)

++ What did the principal do? (He shook Taro's hand.)

++ What did Mrs. Soto and Mrs. Wong give Taro? (a sandwich and hot tea)

+++ What did Taro do next? (He told his story.)

+++ How did Taro's father help him? (He told the story in English.)

+++ How did Taro and his family get home? (The principal drove them.)

+++ What did Taro do before he went to bed? (He took a hot bath.)

++++ Why did Taro say *Ahhh*? (He felt good.)

++++ How did the word *gambaro* help Taro?

++ Do you think Taro will learn English?

+++ Does it help to say to yourself, *It is not easy, but I can do it?*

Activity Sheets

15a. What Happened First? (Stages 1–4)

- Have the students cut the page into sentence strips, mix them up, and arrange them in order to tell the story.

Answers:

1. Taro waited. In two minutes, a police car came.
2. Taro got into the police car.
3. The police took Taro to school.
4. His friends cheered when they saw him. "Hooray! It's Taro! It's Taro!" they shouted.
5. Taro told his story. His father told the story in English.
6. The principal drove Taro and his family to their house.

- Have the students cut on the solid, vertical lines to separate the text from the pictures. Then have them mix up the cards and match the pictures with the sentences.

- Have the students play concentration in pairs or groups of three, matching the sentences with the correct pictures.

- Have the students arrange the pictures in order (without the text) and then write the story in their own words.

15b. Unscramble the Sentences (Stages 2, 3)

- Show the students how to unscramble a sentence. Point out the need for a capital letter at the beginning and a period or question mark at the end. Have the students unscramble the sentences and write them on the lines. Then have them tell who said each one.

Answers:

1. "Can you see a street sign?"/the operator
2. "Are you Taro Yamada?"/the police officer
3. "Thank you so much."/Mrs. Yamada
4. "I am lost."/Taro
5. "Everyone is looking for you."/the police officer
6. "I'll call the police."/the operator

15c. Help Taro Go Home from School (Stages 1–4)

- Have the students start at the Taro symbol and draw a line through the maze to get Taro home. Explain that they cannot cross over any lines. Encourage the students to find the correct path with their fingers before tracing it with their pencils.

Answer:

Here is a logical path. Students' paths may vary slightly.

15d. Write about Taro (Stages 3, 4)

- Teach/review past-tense verb forms in the affirmative and negative. Then have the students compare Taro's life in New York with his life in Japan. Have them read each sentence about his life in Japan and write a sentence about his life in New York.

Answers:

1. But he didn't know how to read in English.
2. But he didn't have (had no) friends in New York / the United States.
3. But he slept on a bed in the United States.
4. But he worried a lot in the United States.
5. But he didn't understand the teachers in the United States.
6. But he didn't know his address in the United States.
7. But he didn't see police officers on every corner in the United States.

- Have the students make up sentences to tell the differences between their former homes and their present homes. If they have never moved, have them write about an imaginary new home or old home.

15e. Match the Sentence Parts (Stages 2, 3)

- Explain that the page contains seven complete sentences, but the students need to find the two parts that go together to make each sentence. Do the first one together as an example. Then have the students match the sentence parts, writing the letter of the best ending on the line next to each sentence beginning.

Answers:

1. c, 2. e, 3. g, 4. a, 5. b, 6. d, 7. f.

- Cover the first column and the letters in the second column before you photocopy this activity. Have the students read the sentences and write the name of the person who best fits each description.

Extension Activities

Total Physical Response: Hooray! It's Taro.
Say and model the following: *Look for Taro. Look up the street. Look down the street. Walk and walk and walk. Call for Taro.* (Taroooo!) *Walk and walk and walk. Look! There he is! Run to him. Hug Taro. He's cold and wet. Put a blanket around him. Give him some hot tea. He's hungry. Give him a sandwich.*

Discovering Grammar. Show the students two different sentence patterns: subject verb object (SVO) and subject, verb, indirect object, object (SVIO). Examples: *Taro's family hugged him.* (SVO) *Mrs. Soto gave him a sandwich. (SVIO)* Have the students identify and create additional sentences in each pattern.

Needs. Ask the students what they think all human beings need. Discuss how people must cooperate to get their needs met. Families provide food, warmth, clothing, shelter, and love for their members, but must rely on farmers, factories, store owners, truck drivers, landlords, government, builders, schools, hospitals, police, and others for many of their other needs.

Acknowledgment and Showing Thanks. Ask: *Why did Taro's friends cheer when they saw him? How do you think that made Taro feel? How did Taro's parents show the other parents how they felt? How can we show our friends that we appreciate and care about them?* Have the students think about the values they get from their families and friends, and how they could acknowledge them. Have the students write thank-you notes to their parents and/or school workers such as custodians, crossing guards, secretary, principal, and nurse. Write a letter to the students to acknowledge their progress, their courage, their questions, their hard work, their persistence, and so on. Have them write to tell you what they like about your lessons and the ways they like to learn. Demonstrate that everyone enjoys acknowledgment and gets good feelings and energy from it.

Pride. Ask the students how Taro felt at the end of the story (proud, happy, relieved). Have them look at his face in panel 15.27. When do your students feel proud of themselves? When do they feel proud of others? How do they show pride? Discuss in pairs or as a class.

CULMINATING ACTIVITIES

1. **Personal Stories.** Have the students write and illustrate stories about their own most dramatic, funny, or interesting experiences. "Publish" the finished products, so the authors may share them with classmates, friends, and family members.

2. **Drama.** Have the students rewrite parts of the story as a play, or create a video drama or puppet show based on the novel. Have the students assume the jobs of role caster and director as well as actors. Eliminate characters if you don't have enough players, and eliminate some of Taro's problems if your time is limited. Invite the students' families or another class to attend the performance.

3. **Welcoming Committee.** Form a committee of students to educate the rest of the school about the problems newcomers face and ways teachers and other students can help. They may want to put up welcome signs in various languages, propose safety rules for the school regarding newcomers, or prepare a "welcome booklet" for newcomers.

4. **Book Reports.** Teach the students common terms used in discussing literature. Have them identify the main character and describe his appearance, his personality, and his strengths and weaknesses. Discuss the answers to the following questions:
   - What secondary characters are there?
   - What problems does the main character have at the beginning of the novel?
   - What does the main character want?
   - What leads up to a bigger problem for Taro?
   - What foreshadows each of these events: the storm, getting lost, the stranger, Taro's determination?
   - How does the author create tension and suspense?
   - How does the author make the story easy to understand?
   - What is the darkest moment of the story?
   - How does the main character solve his problem?
   - Are you satisfied with the ending? Why or why not?
   - What are some of the literary themes in the novel?

   Then have the students write short book reports about the novel.

5. **Skits.** Have the students work in groups to write skits about the common experiences of coming to the United States. Have them perform the skits for the rest of the class or for other classes. Videotape the performances if possible for later viewing and critiquing.

6. **"Wall Magazine."** Have the students create a "Wall Magazine" of their stories and experiences to share with the rest of the school. After the students have written, revised, edited, and shared their work with their classmates, have them "frame" the compositions, draw illustrations, and post their works in the main hall of the school.

7. **Furniture and Floor Plans.** Have the students go through the novel to find the names of rooms and items of furniture (*bedroom, bed, kitchen, table, chair, seat, classroom, desk, chair, bathroom, bathtub*). Have them draw a floor plan of what they think Taro's house looks like, and a floor plan of their own home or the classroom. Teach furniture words as needed: *sofa, armchair, stove, sink, refrigerator, dresser,* and so on.

8. **School and Community Workers.** Discuss and list the types of workers in the story. (*homemaker, mother, teacher, principal, businessman, bus driver, police officers, TV broadcasters*). Can both men and women have these jobs? Who has these jobs in the students' native countries?

9. **Feelings.** What feelings did Taro experience? Review and teach as many as the students are ready for: *happy, curious, surprised, worried, courageous, shy, afraid, appreciative, tired, sick, determined, cold, wet, hopeful, patient, elated, exhausted, relieved, comforted, clean, proud.* Have the students remember a time when they felt one of these feelings and tell a partner or the class about it. Have the students choose four feelings and write a sentence or two about a time when they felt each one.

10. **Evaluation and Critical Thinking.** Point out that all people make mistakes, and it is lucky when we learn from others' mistakes. Discuss the mistakes made by people in the story. (Taro didn't check the bus number, but got on with his classmates; he didn't take his I.D. card; his parents didn't make sure he knew the way home; the school didn't have a plan to help new students; his new friends didn't think about helping him get home; the bus driver wasn't very helpful; and the woman with the small boy didn't try very hard to understand Taro; Taro didn't express his situation to the bus driver; Taro didn't have much money with him; the principal only sent the search party north and east; Taro didn't look for a police officer earlier; the phone company didn't fix its telephone.)

Discuss what happens (or should happen) at your school to prevent new students getting lost. What can you and the students do to help new students become more comfortable in your class?

Ask the students how this story would be different if Taro had come to your school. How would it be different if Taro were from a different country?

Appendix

VOCABULARY LISTED IN ORDER OF APPEARANCE IN THE NOVEL

Note: Both the basic and past forms of a verb are provided in this list, although only one of the forms may appear in the novel.

CHAPTER 1

one
day
a
plane
leave / left
Japan
it
come / came
to
the
United States
boy
is / was
on
his
name
Taro
Yamada
mother
and
sister
are / were
too
Mr.
meet / met
them
at
airport
happy
see / saw
father
Mrs.
Yoko
they

all
get / got
into
taxi
take / took
their
new
home
speak / spoke
in
Japanese
streets
New York
so
wide
say / said
buildings
tall
there
many
different
people
now
we
live / lived
Jackson Heights
will
I
sleep / slept
bed
ask / asked
yes
futon
good night
tomorrow

you
go / went
your
school
stop / stopped
talk / talked

CHAPTER 2

but
can / could
not
he
worry / worried
have / had
friends
no
much
English
make / made
learn / learned
an
American
gambaro
think / thought
easy
do / did
know / knew
alphabet
numbers
hello
goodbye
thank you
for
long
time

then
fall / fell
asleep

CHAPTER 3

next
with
by
bus
junior high
seventh
grade
read / read
books
understand /
    understood
teacher
feel / felt
sick
all
morning
lunchtime
hi
my
Ramón Soto
smile / smiled
point / pointed
himself
another
I'm
am / was
Lee Wong
from
China
this

45

Jae Han Kim
she's
Korea
girl
Susan Bradley
only
one (pron.)
where
doesn't / didn't
hey
that
either
he's
OK
have to / had to
help / helped
him
want / wanted
what
bell
ring / rang
over

CHAPTER 4

afternoon
very
finally
three
o'clock
show / showed
how
get off / got off
when
big
white
gas station
must
work
again
alone
it's
myself
card

identification
address
telephone
I.D. card
keep / kept
pocket
be
careful
don't / didn't
strangers

CHAPTER 5

morning
get up / got up
early
get dressed / got
    dressed
eat / ate
rice
soup
breakfast
turn on / turned
    on
TV
channel 25
news
weather
report
rain / rained
today
weatherman
hard
storm
look / looked
out
window
sunny
clouds
mistake
eight
time
lunch
money

just then
telephone
wait / waited
walk / walked
corner
across
get on / got on

CHAPTER 6

fifteen
minutes
arrive / arrived
difficult
kind
too
fast
copy / copied
words
blackboard
pictures
try / tried
listen / listened
table
sit down / sat
    down
rice balls
lunch box
each
egg roll
taco
apple
half
sandwich
other
Jean-Claude
    Bienami
Haiti
Carmen Lopez
Puerto Rico
Milo Wyborna
Poland
Bao Tran
Vietnam
all

CHAPTER 7

good
math
need / needed
gym
at last
outside
cloudy
windy
right
bus stop
baseball
throw / threw
catch / caught
back
play / played
ball
soon
everyone
next to
short
bye
stop /stopped
every
gone
on and on

CHAPTER 8

uh oh
maybe
wrong
bus driver
something
dark
wind
blow / blew
papers
cans
call / called
put / put
oh, no!
lost
city
third

CHAPTER 9

walking (walk /
   walked)
quickly
woman
small
away
darker
harder
two
short
tall
take / took
three
seven
ten
begin / began
wet
place
stay / stayed
dry
under
stairs
run / ran
there
running
bad
cars
turn on / turned
   on
lights
even
lake
head
book bag
shoes
socks
feet

CHAPTER 10

three-thirty
four-thirty
where
principal
answer / answered
calls
husband
forget / forgot
right there

CHAPTER 11

students
class
know / knew
need / needed
a lot
tell / told
parents
police
glad
look like / looked
   like
officer
twelve
years old
four
eleven
inches
straight
black
hair
eyes
wearing (wear /
   wore)
shirt
blue
sweater
jeans
green
jacket

carrying (carry /
   carried)
here
picture
stations

CHAPTER 12

still
slow / slowed
nod / nodded
no one
right
bigger
start / started
blocks
tired
hungry
cold
cry / cried
man
crying
remember /
   remembered
should

CHAPTER 13

meanwhile
bring / brought
grandmother
map
north
east
our
us
show / showed
nine
ten
if
find
about
ten-fifteen

CHAPTER 14

policeman /
   policemen
broken
pick / picked
wonder / wondered
fingers
shaking (shake /
   shook)
press / pressed
voice
operator
hooray
moshi moshi
moment

CHAPTER 15

sign
can't
letters
seventy-three
Grand Street
police car
blanket
around
warm
ahhh
cheer / cheered
shout / shouted
hug / hugged
shake / shook
hot
tea
tell / told
story
drive / drove
bath

VOCABULARY LISTED ALPHABETICALLY

Note: Both the basic and past forms of a verb are provided in this list, although only one of the forms may appear in the novel.

A

a
a lot of
about
across
address
afternoon
again
ahhh
airport
all
alone
alphabet
am
American
and
another
answer
apple
are
around
arrive / arrived
ask / asked
asleep
at
at last
away

B

back
bad
ball
Bao Tran
baseball
bath
be
bed
begin / began

bell
big
bigger
black
blackboard
blanket
blocks
blow / blew
blue
book bag
books
boy
breakfast
bring / brought
broken
buildings
bus
bus driver
bus stop
but
by
bye

C

call / called
can / could
cans
can't
card
careful
Carmen Lopez
carrying (carry / carried)
cars
catch / caught
channel
cheer / cheered
China

city
class
clouds
cloudy
cold
come / came
copy / copied
corner
cry / cried
crying

D

dark
darker
day
didn't
different
difficult
do / did
doesn't / didn't
don't / didn't
down
drive / drove
dry

E

each
early
east
easy
eat / ate
egg roll
eight
either
eleven
English
even
every

everyone
eyes

F

fall / fell
fast
father
feel / felt
feet / foot
finally
find / found
fingers
forget / forgot
four-thirty
friends
from
futon

G

gambaro
gas station
get / got dressed
get / got off
get / got on
get / got up
girl
glad
go / went
gone
good
good night
goodbye
grade
Grand Street
grandmother
green
gym

H

hair
Haiti
half
happy
hard
harder
have / had
have to / had to
he
head
hello
help / helped
here
hey
hi
him
himself
his
home
hooray
hot
how
hug / hugged
hungry
husband

I

I
identification
I.D. card
if
I'm
in
inches
into
is / was
it

J

jacket
Jackson Heights
Jae Han Kim
Japan
Japanese
Jean-Claude
  Bienami
jeans
junior high
just then

K

keep / kept
kind
know / knew
Korea

L

lake
learn / learned
leave / left
Lee Wong
letters
lights
listen / listened
live / lived
long
look / looked
look like / looked
  like
lost
lunch
lunch box
lunchtime

M

make / made
man
many
map
math
meanwhile
meet / met
Milo Wynorna
minutes
mistake
moment
money
morning
moshi moshi
mother
Mr.
Mrs.
much
must
my
myself

N

name
need / needed
new
New York (City)
news
next
next to
nine
no
no one
nod / nodded
north
not
now
numbers

O

o'clock
officer
oh, no!
OK
on
on and on
one
only
operator
our
out
outside
over

P

papers
parents
people
phone
pick / picked
pictures
place
plane
play / played
pocket
point / pointed
Poland
police
police car
policeman
policemen
press / pressed
principal
Puerto Rico
put

Q

quickly

R

rain / rained
Ramón Soto
ran / run
read / read
remember /
  remembered
report
rice
rice balls
right
right there
ring / rang
running (run / ran)

S

sandwich
say / said

school
see / saw
seven
seventh
seventy-third
shake / shook
shaking
she
shirt
shoes
short
should
shout / shouted
show / showed
sick
sign
sister
sit / sat
sleep / slept
slow / slowed
small
smile / smiled
so
socks
something
soon
soup
speak / spoke
stairs
start / started
station
stay / stayed
still

stop / stopped
storm
story
straight
strangers
street
students
sunny
Susan Bradley
sweater

T

table
taco
take / took
talk / talked
tall
Taro
taxi
tea
teacher
telephone
tell / told
ten-fifteen
thank you
that
the
their
them
there
they
think / thought
thirty

this
three
three-thirty
throw / threw
time
tired
to
today
tomorrow
too
try / tried
turn on / turned
on
TV
twelve
two

U

uh oh
under
understand /
understood
United States
us

V

very
Vietnam
voice

W

wait / waited
walk / walked

walking
want / wanted
warm
was / were
we
wearing (wear /
wore)
weather
weatherman
wet
what
when
where
white
wide
will
window
wind
windy
with
woman
wonder / wondered
words
work / worked
worried
wrong

Y

Yamada
years old
yes
Yoko
you
your

Reproducible Activity Sheets

Note: There is a small lightbulb icon ( ) in the lower right-hand margin of each Activity Sheet. This icon gives the page number in the Guide on which you can find additional teaching suggestions and answers.

Here is a list of the *Where Is Taro?* Activity Sheets:

1a   Listen and Circle
1b   What Do You See?
1c   What Happened First?
1d   Tell a Story
1e   Interview a Partner

2a   Listen and Circle
2b   Complete the Sentences
2c   What Worried You?

3a   Listen and Circle
3b   What Do You See?
3c   What Are They Saying?

4a   Listen and Circle
4b   What Are They Saying?
4c   Complete the I.D. Cards

5a   Listen and Circle
5b   What Do You See?
5c   Tell about Your Morning

6a   Listen and Circle
6b   Choose the Best Sentence
6c   Complete the Sentences

7a   Listen and Circle
7b   What Are They Doing?
7c   What Happened First?

Listen and Circle

Name _____   Date _____

What Do You See?

1. Taro   <u> E </u>

2. Taro's mother   _____

3. Taro's father   _____

4. Taro's sister   _____

5. taxi   _____

6. plane   _____

7. home   _____

8. street   _____

Name _____   Date _____

What Happened First?

Cut on the dotted lines. Put the sentences in order.

The family got into a taxi.

Mr. Yamada came to the airport to meet them.

One day, a plane left Japan and came to the United States.

Mrs. Yamada was on the plane with Taro and Yoko.

The taxi took them to their new home.

The children were happy to see their father.

WHERE IS TARO TEACHER'S KIT by Elizabeth Claire. Copyright © 1995 by Harcourt Brace & Company. All rights reserved.

16

Name _____ Date _____

Tell a Story

1.

One day a _____ came to

_____ .

2.

A _____ was on the

_____ .

3.

_____ name was

_____ .

4.

_____'s _____

and _____ were on

the _____ , too.

Name _____   Date _____

17

Interview a Partner

Ask your partner these questions. You can ask other questions, too. Listen to your partner's answers. Then, your partner will ask you questions.

1. Where were you born?
2. When did you come to _____ (this country / this city)?
3. How did you get here?
4. Who came with you?
5. How was the (plane) trip? Do you remember anything special about the trip?
6. Did anyone meet you at the _____ (airport / train station)?
7. Was anyone in your family already in this country?
8. Were you happy to come here? Why or why not?
9. What things did you bring with you?
10. What things did you leave in your old home?
11. Who did not come with you?
12. Will other people in your family come here, too?

WHERE IS TARO TEACHER'S KIT by Elizabeth Claire. Copyright © 1995 by Harcourt Brace & Company. All rights reserved.

17

Name _____ Date _____

Listen and Circle

1. a. 	b. 	(c.) 	d. 
2. a. 	b. 	c. 	d. 
3. a. 	b. 	c. 	d. 
4. a. **8**	b. **11**	c. **12**	d. **9**
5. a. **e**	b. **h**	c. **g**	d. **y**
6. a. 	b. 	c. 	d. 

Name _____ Date _____

Complete the Sentences

1. Taro could not _____ sleep _____ .

2. In Japan, he had many _____ .

3. He could not _____ much English.

4. "It is not easy," he thought, "but _____ can do it."

5. "I know the _____ in English."

6. "I know the _____ ."

WORD BANK					
alphabet	friends	sleep ✔	speak	numbers	I

Name _____ Date _____

19

What Worried You?

no friends

Name _____ Date _____

Listen and Circle

Name _____   Date _____

ACTIVITY
3b

What Do You See?

1. desk ___E___
2. boy _____
3. girl _____
4. book _____
5. paper _____
6. blackboard _____
7. window _____
8. chair _____
9. teacher _____

21

Name _____ Date _____

What Are They Saying?

1.

   I'm Lee Wong.

   I'm from China.

2.

3.

4.

5. Draw your picture here. What are you saying?

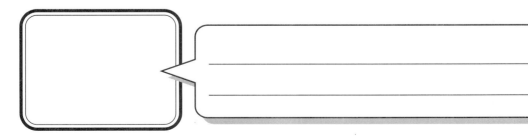

Name _____ Date _____

Listen and Circle

1. a. b.  c.  (d.)

2. a.  b.  c.  d.

3. a. 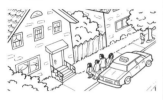 b.  c.  d.

4. a.  b.  c.  d.

5. a.  b.  c.  d.

6. a. Address 4472 29th Street Jackson Heights New York, N.Y. 11379   b. Telephone (718) 555-2121   c. Name Taro Yamada   d. IDENTIFICATION Name Taro Yamada Address 4472 29th Street Jackson Heights New York, N.Y. 11379 Telephone (718) 555-2121

23

Name _____   Date _____

What Are They Saying?

1.

I must go to **work** _____ tomorrow.

2.

_____
_____
_____
_____
Yoko.

3.

It _____ _____ _____ , but _____ _____ _____ _____ .

4.

This _____ _____ I.D. card. _____ _____ _____ _____ pocket.

Name _____ Date _____

Complete the I.D. Cards

1. Make your identification card.

IDENTIFICATION

First name _____ Last name _____

Address _____

_____

_____

Telephone _____

---

2. Make an identification card for Ramón.

IDENTIFICATION

Ramón _____ Soto _____

First name _____ Last name _____

Address _____

11379

City _____ State _____ Zip code _____

Telephone _____

Ramón Soto

24

Name _____ Date _____

Listen and Circle

Name _____   Date _____

25

What Do You See?

1. rice   **E**

2. soup   _____

3. TV   _____

4. money   _____

5. telephone   _____

6. window   _____

7. lunch   _____

8. I.D. card   _____

Name _____ Date _____

Tell about Your Morning

Cut on the dotted lines. Put the sentences in order.

I eat breakfast.

I go to school.

I brush my teeth.

I comb my hair.

I get dressed.

I get up.

Name _____ Date _____

26

Listen and Circle

Name _____ Date _____

Choose the Best Sentence

1. (a.) Lee and Ramón were at the table.

   b. Lee and Ramón were at the desk.

2. a. There were eight apples in Taro's lunch box.

   b. There were eight rice balls in Taro's lunch box.

3. a. Taro gave Ramón a taco.

   b. Ramón gave Taro a taco.

4. a. Taro smiled. He had new friends.

   b. Taro smiled. He had eight rice balls.

Name _____ Date _____

Complete the Sentences

The morning was difficult. The _____ teachers _____ were kind, but
(1)

they _____ too fast. Taro said to himself, "It is not easy,
(2)

In 1860, the U.S. had a new president, Abraham Lincoln.

but _____ can do it." He copied _____
(3)   (4)

from the blackboard. He looked at the _____ in his books.
(5)

He tried to _____ to the teacher. He waited for
(6)

_____ .
(7)

WORD BANK

words   pictures   lunchtime   I   teachers ✔   listen   talked

---

Name _____   Date _____

 28

Listen and Circle

Name _____   Date _____

What Are They Doing?

1. <u>He is throwing</u>
    <u>the ball.</u>

2. _____

3. _____

4. _____

5. _____

6. _____

WORD BANK

He	is	getting on	the bus.
She	are	getting off	the ball.
They		throwing	
		catching	
		sitting on	
		waiting for	

Name _____   Date _____

What Happened First?

Cut on the dotted lines. Put the sentences in order.

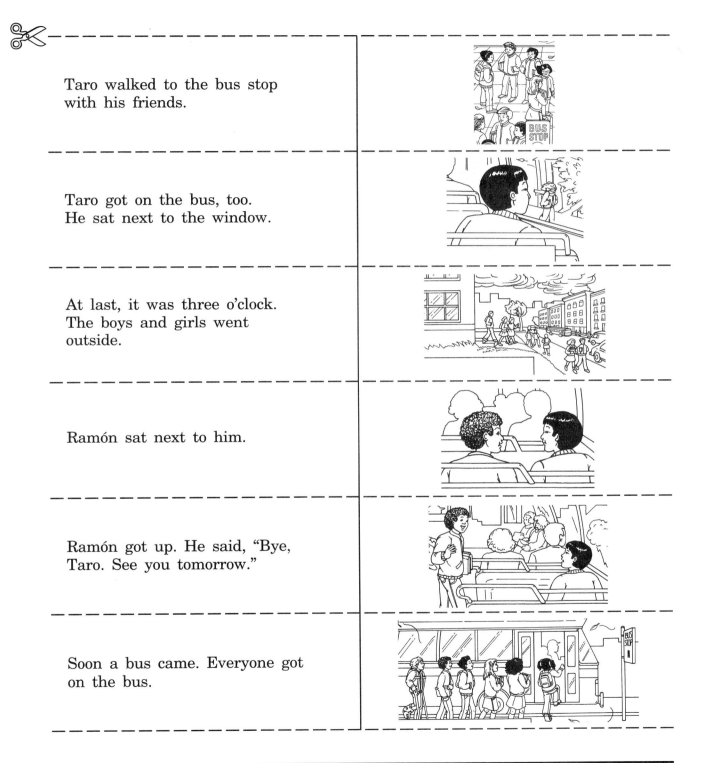

Taro walked to the bus stop with his friends.

Taro got on the bus, too. He sat next to the window.

At last, it was three o'clock. The boys and girls went outside.

Ramón sat next to him.

Ramón got up. He said, "Bye, Taro. See you tomorrow."

Soon a bus came. Everyone got on the bus.

Name _____   Date _____

ACTIVITY

8a

Listen and Circle

Name _____   Date _____

What Do You See?

ACTIVITY

8b

1.	woman	_E_	4.	bus	_____	
2.	book bag	_____	5.	bus stop	_____	
3.	school	_____	6.	car	_____	

7.	cloud	_____
8.	bus driver	_____
9.	ball	_____

Name _____   Date _____

What Do You See?

ACTIVITY
8b

1. woman	_E_	4. bus	_____	7. cloud	_____
2. book bag	_____	5. bus stop	_____	8. bus driver	_____
3. school	_____	6. car	_____	9. ball	_____

Name _____   Date _____

Listen and Circle

Name _____ Date _____

Make New Conversations

Does this bus go to
Jackson Heights ?

No, it doesn't.

The number
three bus.

Which bus goes to
Jackson Heights ?

WORD BANK

Place	Bus number
Manhattan	eleven
Central Park	two
Franklin High School	ten
Thirty-fourth Street	six
Main Street	one

Name _____ Date _____

Ask for and Give Directions

Work with a partner to complete the map. First, read the information in the box.

> You are A, and your partner is B. You each have a map. Cut out the eight little
> pictures at the bottom of the page. Put the A pictures in the A squares on your map.
> B puts the B pictures on his or her map. Don't show each other your maps! Now ask
> your partner how to get to the B places. Here is an example:
>
> **A: How do I get to the post office?**
> **B: Go two blocks on Center Street. The post office is on your right.**
>
> Follow B's directions and put your post office picture in the correct square.
>   Take turns asking for and giving directions. Then look at the two maps together.
> Are they the same?

B   B   A

Twenty-seventh Street

A   B   A

Twenty-eighth Street

B   A

Twenty-ninth Street

You are here.

Main Street
Street
Center
Market Street

A: WASHINGTON SCHOOL   A: BUS STOP   A: BANK   A: SUPERMARKET   B: (phone)   B: POST OFFICE   B: GAS STATION   B: POLICE STATION

WHERE IS TARO TEACHER'S KIT by Elizabeth Claire. Copyright © 1995 by Harcourt Brace & Company. All rights reserved.

 33

Name _____   Date _____

What Are They Saying?

1.

It's four-thirty.
Where is Taro?

2.

3.

4.

IDENTIFICATION
Name Taro Yamada
Address 4472 29th Street
Jackson Heights
New York, N.Y. 11379
Telephone (718) 555-2121

Name _____ Date _____

Unscramble the Words

At (**rheet-tyhirt**) _____three-thirty_____ , Mrs. Yamada and Yoko went to
(1)

the big white (**sga ttainos**) _____ _____ .
(2)

They (**detawi**) _____ for Taro's bus.
(3)

(**yman**) _____ buses came, but Taro was not on any bus. At
(4)

four-thirty, it (**gnabe**) _____ to rain. Mrs. Yamada and Yoko
(5)

were (**rewordi**) _____ . They went back to their
(6)

(**shuoe**) _____ .
(7)

Name _____   Date _____

Read and Color

This is Milo. Milo is from Poland. He's in the seventh grade. Milo and Taro are friends.

Milo has short, straight blond hair and blue eyes. He is wearing a yellow shirt and a red sweater. He is wearing blue jeans and black shoes. He is carrying an orange book bag. It is raining very hard. Milo is also carrying a purple umbrella.

Name _____ Date _____

Play a Guessing Game

Play this game with your classmates. One person picks a face. Which face is it? Find out by asking five yes/no questions. Whoever guesses correctly then picks the next face. Here are some example questions and answers.

1. Student A: Does she have short hair?   Student B: No.
2. Student C: Is she wearing glasses?   Student B: Yes.
3. Student D: Does she have curly hair?   Student B: No.
4. Student E: Does she have blonde hair?   Student B: Yes.
5. Student F: Is it Kari?   Student B: Yes!

1. Anna 2. Susan 3. Olga 4. Tova

5. Jae Han 6. Akiko 7. Carmen 8. Tina

9. Bao 10. Marilyn 11. Judy 12. Jackie

13. Betty 14. Kari 15. Rosa 16. Dani

 35

Name _____   Date _____

Describe Yourself

Talk about Yourself

Talk with a partner. Take turns asking and answering these questions.

1. How old are you?
2. What do you look like?
3. How tall are you?

4. Do you wear glasses?
5. What are you wearing?

Write about Yourself

Complete the paragraph.

I'm _____ years old. I'm _____ feet,

_____ inches tall. I have _____ ,

_____ _____ hair and _____

eyes. I _____ wear glasses. Today, I'm wearing

_____

_____

_____ .

Draw Yourself

WHERE IS TARO TEACHER'S KIT by Elizabeth Claire. Copyright © 1995 by Harcourt Brace & Company. All rights reserved.

36

Name _____ Date _____

Choose the Best Sentence

1. a. The bus was coming. Taro had more money in his pocket.

   (b.) The bus was gone. Taro didn't have money for another bus.

2. a. Taro was very wet and hungry.

   b. Taro was very wet and happy.

3. a. Taro wanted to cry, but he didn't cry.

   b. Taro didn't want to cry, but he cried.

4. a. Taro saw a man crying. He spoke to the man.

   b. A man saw Taro crying. He spoke to Taro.

5. a. Taro remembered his father's words, "Don't talk to strangers."

   b. Taro remembered the stranger's words, "Don't cry."

Name _____ Date _____

How Are the Pictures Different?

Find **eight** differences. Circle them.

A.

B.

WHERE IS TARO TEACHER'S KIT by Elizabeth Claire. Copyright © 1995 by Harcourt Brace & Company. All rights reserved.

Name _____ Date _____

Play a Guessing Game

water	soup	sandwich	police officer
taxi	book	pencil	bed
apple	cold	hungry	tired
worried	happy	telephone	money

WHERE IS TARO TEACHER'S KIT by Elizabeth Claire. Copyright © 1995 by Harcourt Brace & Company. All rights reserved.

38

Name _____   Date _____

Draw and Guess

Play this game in a small group. First, cut the words apart. Turn them over and put them in a pile. One classmate picks a word and draws a picture of that word. The other students in the group try to guess the word. Take turns. How quickly can your group guess all the words?

bus driver	chair	bell
three o'clock	rice	TV
rain storm	lunch	gym
window	pocket	principal
map	gas station	woman
jacket	stairs	clouds
building	corner	people

Name _____ Date _____

Unscramble and Match the Opposites

1. tew

    <u>   wet   </u>

    a. trosh

    _____

2. slaml

    _____

    b. gebni

    _____

3. solt

    _____

    c. tewn

    _____

4. pots

    _____

    d. grensart

    _____

5. latl

    _____

    e. ryd

    <u>   dry   </u>

6. drinfe

    _____

    f. ibg

    _____

7. meac

    _____

    g. tucfidfil

    _____

8. yase

    _____

    h. onduf

    _____

Name _____ Date _____

39

Use the Telephone

coin slot

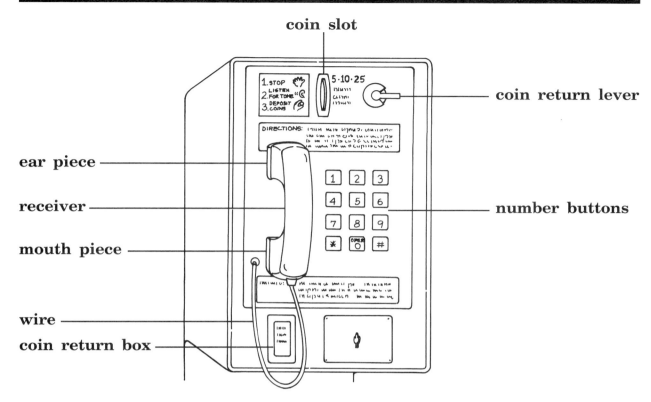

ear piece

receiver

mouth piece

wire

coin return box

coin return lever

number buttons

Read the sentences. Fill in the blanks with words about the telephone.

1. Pick up the _____receiver_____. Listen for a dial tone.

2. Deposit your coins in the _____ _____.

3. Dial your number. Press the _____ _____.
   You don't need the area code for a local call.

4. If you hear a "beep beep beep" the line is busy. Hang up.

5. If the line is busy or no one answers, press the _____
   _____ _____. Get your money back in the
   _____ _____ _____.

6. If you need help, press "0" for operator.

Name _____ Date _____

Practice the Conversations

Operator 1: This is Michael. May I help you?

Taro: I don't know my phone number.

Operator 1: Dial 411 for Information.

Operator 2: What city, please?

Taro: Jackson Heights, please. I want the number for Kenji Yamada.

Operator 2: Can you spell that last name, please?

Taro: Y-A-M-A-D-A.

Operator 2: Thank you. Here's your number.

Computer voice: The number is area code 718-555-1234.

Operator 3: This is Rosa. May I help you?

Taro: I don't have any money for the telephone.

Operator 3: You can call collect. What number do you want?

Taro: 555-1234.

Operator 3: What is your name, please?

Taro: Taro.

(Ring. Ring. Ring.)

Mrs. Yamada: Hello.

Operator 3: You have a collect call from Taro. Will you accept the charges?

Mrs. Yamada: Yes, I will. Hello, Taro? Where are you?

Name _____ Date _____

What Happened First?

Cut on the dotted lines. Put the sentences in order.

His friends cheered when they saw him. "Hooray! It's Taro! It's Taro!" they shouted.

The police took Taro to his school.

Taro told his story. His father told the story in English.

Taro got into the police car.

The principal drove Taro and his family to their house.

Taro waited. In two minutes, a police car came.

Name _____   Date _____

Unscramble the Sentences

Write the correct sentence on the line. Then tell who said it.

the operator   **Mrs. Yamada**   **Taro**   **the police officer**

1. "see street a can sign you?"

   "Can you see a street sign?"

   Who said it? _____ the operator _____

2. "Taro are Yamada you?"

   _____

   Who said it? _____

3. "much you thank so."

   _____

   Who said it? _____

4. "lost am I."

   _____

   Who said it? _____

5. "you is looking everyone for."

   _____

   Who said it? _____

6. "the I'll police call."

   _____

   Who said it? _____

Name _____   Date _____

Help Taro Go Home from School

42

Name _____   Date _____

Write about Taro

1. Taro knew how to read in Japanese.
   But he didn't know how to read in English.

2. Taro had many friends in Japan.

3. Taro slept on a futon in Japan.

4. Taro didn't worry a lot in Japan.

5. Taro understood the teachers in Japan.

6. Taro knew his address in Japan.

7. Taro saw police officers on every corner in Japan.

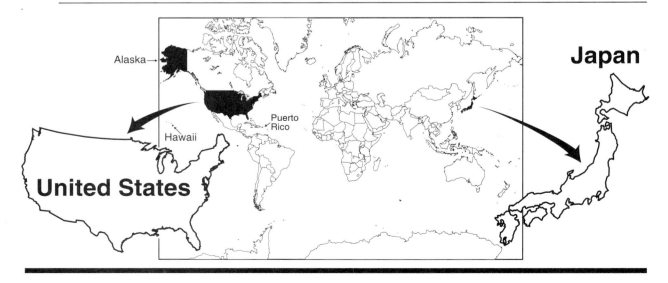

Alaska →

Puerto Rico

Hawaii

United States

Japan

WHERE IS TARO TEACHER'S KIT by Elizabeth Claire. Copyright © 1995 by Harcourt Brace & Company. All rights reserved.

42

Name _____ Date _____

Match the Sentence Parts

1. A grandmother ___C___   a. drives a bus.

2. A principal _____   b. is a person you do not know.

3. A police officer _____   c. is the mother of a mother or father.

4. A bus driver _____   d. is a mother or father.

5. A stranger _____   e. is a person who manages a school.

6. A parent _____   f. works for the telephone company.

7. An operator _____   g. helps people when there is trouble or an accident.

42

Name _____   Date _____

NOTES

NOTES